Symptom and Desire

Also by Lyman Grant

Poetry:
2018: Found Poems and Weather Reports
Old Men on Tuesday Mornings
Last Work: A Meditation on the Final Paintings of Neal Adams
As Long as We Need
Established Parameters
The Road Home
Text & Commentary

Works Edited:
Writing Texas 4
Writing Texas 3
New Growth: Contemporary Short Fiction by Texas Writers
The Letters of Roy Bedichek (with William A. Owens)

Textbooks:
Short Fiction: Classic and Contemporary (with Charles Bohner)
CommonSense: A Handbook for Writers (with Lennis Polnac and Tom Cameron)

Magazine:
MAN!

Symptom and Desire

New and Selected Poems

By
Lyman Grant

Four Door Lounge

Symptom and Desire: New and Selected Poems
copyright © 2023 by Lyman Grant
All rights reserved.

Cover Design: 4doorloungebooks
Cover Art: by Neal Adams
"The Dying Leaves"
2005
Ink, oil sticks, and dried flowers on paper
40"x 30.25"
used by permission of the Neal Adams Estate

Published by 4doorloungebooks
33 East Weaver Ave.
Harrisonburg, VA 22801
www.4doorlounge.com
4doorloungbooks@gmail.com

ISBN: 979-8-9872180-4-4

To my parents
Lyman Winstead Grant, Sr.
And Birdie Louise Jamison Grant

Table of Contents

1. from *Text & Commentary* — 5
   - Hairetikos — 7
   - The Dying Leaves — 8
   - Education by Fire — 9
   - Love Song from Country of Memory — 11
   - Cancer — 13
   - Grieving for My Parents — 14
   - The Drawing — 15
   - Planting Shrubs — 16
   - The Garden — 17
   - The Light through the Peaks — 18
   - The Open Hand — 20
   - Found Things — 22
   - Endings — 23

2. from *The Road Home* — 25
   - Voyager — 27
   - Searching the Parking Lot for a Poem — 29
   - The Rose's Thorns — 31
   - 290 West — 33
   - Absolution — 35
   - "Hamlet" — 36
   - Black Bowl with Apples on Old Table Cloth — 38
   - Ark — 39
   - If You Should Ever Return — 40
   - The Way Things Go — 41
   - Soul Mates — 42
   - These are things I've been wanting to tell you — 43
   - An Animal Speaks of Speaking on Christmas Day — 45
   - Late Night — 47
   - The Angel of Santa Maria — 48
   - Setting Them Down — 49
   - A Dream of Grace — 50
   - More Metaphors — 51
   - The Laying on of Hands — 52

3. from *As Long as We Need* 53
   Midlife Christmas 55
   Six Motets 56
   Product Reliability 58
   Listening and Knowing Where to Look 59
   The Other Writers Block 60
   Dark Night on Deck Upstairs 62
   After Hades, Always Persephone 63
   Weekend Forecast 64
   Dawning 65
   Ice Storm 66
   Mirror Stage 68
   Burn Ban 71
   The Upper Room 73
   This Easter 75
   It is not that I 76
   Sometimes I cannot 78
   Lord, Remember 79
   Midnight 80
   Always 81
   Fall in America 82
   Speed Limit 83
   Safe House 84

4. Uncollected Poems 85
   Pedestal 87
   Spring 89
   The Lure 91
   Scene from the Movie *Diva* 92
   Summer Returns to Texas 94
   The Tab 95
   Three Teslas 97
   Mayberry Sequence 99
   The High Shelf 103

5.	from *Last Work*	105
6.	from *Old Men on Tuesday Mornings*	111
	Old Men on Tuesday Morning	113
	Ode American	114
	Little Storm	121
	Arroyo Sunset	122
	Deep End	123
	Heirlooms	124
	Open Carry	125
	From What Planet	127
	Small Bird	128
	Ghost Story	129
	Bio	130
7.	from *2018: Found Poems and Weather Reports*	131
	January 23	133
	February 14	134
	April 22	135
	May 3	136
	June 21	137
	July 24	139
	September 16	140
	October 25	141
	November 18	143
8.	New Poems	145
	Symptomatic	147
	The Age of Misgiving	148
	Ambition	149
	The Dream	150
	Lists	151
	Knot	152
	Algorithm	153
	SOS	154
	Mirror	155
	Half/Full	156

Evacuation	157
Art	158
Perusing Hugo	160
Ransom	161
Dude for a Day	162
Epithalamium	164
Tourist Trade	166
What He Knows of Sunlight	167
Sacrificial	168
Holding On	169
Cloudy Day	170
Toward Atonement	172
Acknowledgements	175
The Author	178

Symptom and Desire

There is no subject without a symptom.
    Jacques Lacan, *Seminar 23*

We are always asking the Other what he desires.
    Jacques Lacan, *My Teaching*

from
Text & Commentary

Hairetikos

Make me a weed,
a wild and restless thing,
too burning for a flaming sky
to green myself in shade.

Make me a weed,
with roots as thin as sparks,
with leaves that dance in summer heat
like campfires on a plain.

Make me a weed,
the strider of the squall,
strange tower above rooted grass,
an iceberg overturned.

Make me a weed,
browned and dried by flame,
charred and withered from fires within,
an ash on earth's hot brow.

The Dying Leaves
For Neal Adams

My friend wants to cut them off,
but I believe that nature can
decide to drop these yellow leaves
when plant and leaves will amiably part.

As in drawings, I like dark and light
to hesitate. I like lingering lines
that fade where line and page are one.
My friend likes dark lines that define.

I want a leisurely look and life.
He thinks life is work and must be
paid for everyday: I will die
of long disease, my friend of heart attack.

Education by Fire

He touched the fire.
Well, not fire exactly,
but those blood red coals
that burn below the cool
gray ashes of dying fires,
a two-inch cruelty
he tumbled through.

Tomorrow, calm as a surgeon,
a curious geographer
in a strange, harsh land,
he inspects his blisters,
large as bites of bubble gum
stuck to every finger,

but tonight, his hand,
globbed in Silvadene,
loosely wrapped in gauze
and wrapped again
in an old brown Ace
looks like a half-cooked drumstick,
the skin sliced away.
His arm has become the baseball
bat he may never grip.

We don't know yet.

Parents like to nurse their pain
at their child's expense,
but looking at his hand
exposed in the hospital glare
all five helpless fingers

erect and swollen, white from heat
and dripping skin,
made me want to scream.

His screams were not loud enough,
for I can never know the pain
that this astonished hand
educated in my son tonight.

Love Song from the Country of Memory

The gate at the bottom of the hill
was opened for us, and two tracks,
grass short and lush between,
(that which separates defines them)
gracefully curved up the hill
toward your dead uncle's home,

past a pond, the still water enveloped,
but enveloping, too, an island doll house,
a copy as tangible as the object
it is the mirror of.

Midday in spring,
cows crowd the fence
near the curving drive,
their udders growing full,
and flowers (I still cannot name them)
clump color and lean our way,
last survivors of the cows' long tongues.
You warn me that the cellar has bees
and to stay away or else.

I stay away
and walk down to the pond.

As a girl you used to row across
this pond to play house.
(Your uncle warned you of the snakes.)
The boat has sunk, they say,
but I see you then,
my country girl, no Victorian bows,
your thick brown curls blow across your face,

your rural cotton dress undulates.
It rises and falls like waves on the pond.
(What did your uncle think
from his front porch,
spying on your billowing girlhood?)
Yes, I see you,
your thin, thin fingers
delicately arranging your furniture and your dolls.

You see, Mama,
I remember these things you told me
as we walked hand in hand around that pond.
The frogs dove in from the shore.

Now I half expect your tender face
to rise from the waters of my dreams.
I will gently lean to kiss your lips
but fall and drown.
That little house will shake,
the water moan.

Cancer

The wheelchair waits beside the Christmas tree,
one of those cheap firs from Safeway, thin,
spindly, dropping its needles on the carpet.
In the wheelchair is my mother,
wrapped in a fading housecoat of spring flowers,
so small and pale. The threads fall from their dull petals.
Her gray hair hangs like tinsel from the five and dime.
She is as fragile as the last antique ornament,
a small country church covered in snow. From its steeple
it hangs by one thin wire and a bending branch.
She is forty-six and looks like ninety.
She waits beside the tree like a dove
for the sound of footsteps in the fallen leaves.

Grieving for My Parents

Ashes float on the pond behind our home.
It's here we prayed for her return.
Year on year, we skimmed the leaves
the giant oak had spread,
searching for her face beneath our own.
Then another leaf dropped,

and the water breathed. One wave became
the flood. Frogs hurled themselves
upon our lawn. Our frightened pets
barked and pawed at the furless beasts,
fugitives in both their homes.
Then the miracle occurred.

The dragon leaped from the lapping water
and growled like grandpa's razor strop.
Snap! The cats and dogs went down
with frogs between their teeth.
Snap! I lost a leg and crawled
beneath the house to hide.

Before she pulled herself back to the bottom,
she growled again and covered
the giant oak in flame. We watched
him burn for days before
his collapse into the calm, accepting pond.
I have a tube now

in my chest that drains a fluid bodies
don't contain. The ashes never go away.
They drift in winds I cannot feel
on a surface I cannot see.
The doctors say I should stay inside.
I do not know how deep those waters go.

The Drawing

Our son has jabbed the sheet
I was writing on
and named it rain.
A tight-fisted deeply
pressed slash of black
that looks like an ancient
word—this is his lightning.
A smooth curve that bends
itself off the page
and back, knotting tightly
then fading, somewhat
like your summer ponytail,
is not the moon
as I guessed but thunder.

Of course.
To those who are not parents
sounds still have shape.
I howl in the gash
I axed in our strongest oak.
You gasp, frightened,
from the gaping soil
where your clippers fell.

I fear, my love,
I have forgotten
how to draw the moan
my heart makes in full
satisfaction of its
love for you. Our son
is right. This page is air
in an August storm.
My heart speaks like
a lost letter rejoined
to a word whispered
late at night.

Planting Shrubs

You do this for beauty
and order and Sunday afternoons
when family sit in shady
lawns eating smoky meats,
potato salad, and Jell-O,
the color of blood.

Here, at least, perfection
is possible. Line
and distance can be measured,
short branches clipped
for summer growth. These
ideas rest your mind

until the point refuses
to sink: dull joy dies
as shovel tip crumbles
into God's stone.
On your knees you measure
growth in scoops of dirt

in gloved hands. You
are a stranger here
where root and rock ask
no forgiveness from serene
reality. Give up.
Plant where random

tenderness allows.
Let meat eaters frown.
Trust the wild lines
you cannot see. Devils
dance when muscles
turn to stone.

The Garden

My garden is filled,
not with roses or corn,
not with songs
of sparrows in low branches,
but with Cambodian statues,
and wild foliage that never blooms
but sends its wet tentacles
up and around stone bodies
like screams. The clamor of rot
and broken limbs echoes in the mists
and the lush hardwood canopies.
There, in each hidden wing beat
I hear the deathless urge
toward retreat. I lie naked
in the moist leaves, vines
tightening around my waist,
and rest my head, crazed
with dreams, on scattered
hands from broken gods.

The Light through the Peaks

1.
One night your wife won't turn to you
through the dark and you start
a war in another country.
Bombs go off in your father's arms;
the light is immense but you must look.
Your son is thrown to the bottom
of a deep well, but you have
no buckets to save him,
for you have turned them into guns.

In one sleepless night,
you have learned how the world ends.

2.
The dark moon follows her own course.
Turn the other way.

3.
A middle-aged man shouts at the mother
who died when he was away at school.
He stares at the mountains in hate.
The angry man cries because his mother
went insane. He has no one now to slap
while his father speeds on to emergency wards.
The old man with kids our age
has not left his mother for the tides.
His children laugh at him like a fisherman
who returns home with empty nets.

4.
The earth cannot hold all their tears.
No matter where they fall,
they return to the blazing sea.
The tides will turn or not turn,
but there will be no more tears in you:

This is how the world begins.
Light rises through the peaks.

The Open Hand
for William A. Owens (1905-1990)

1.
Though the hand of the giver remains
open, forever releasing claim, something
remains attached. Perhaps it is light
from his fingers, or breath from his
sweet lips, perhaps a song he hummed
into the wrapping. And the hand
that receives stays forever open,
shining, scented, singing, passing gifts
to other trembling, tentative hands.

2.
The land is vast, and trails rise
high into mountains, far above
the muddy rivers to a great meadow
that wild goats may find before
they die. They braid their musky hair
in bright beads and wear wreaths
of red columbine. They are given
shoots of tender grass. Morning mists
return in bright afternoon rains.

3.
Bill, this land I walk will never
be mine alone, I know now, nor
has it ever been since you
revealed to me what I already held.
Each print I leave in mud,
sand, or red clay holds, too,
the press of your weight. The urge
in my step rose when you showed me
the trail I feared to find.

4.
If men were true, we would not
speak of our love with words like
mentor, comrade, friend. They bear
no relation to the rivers and soils,
which nurture in us everlasting
acts of giving and accepting.
You have drifted away, an animal
into dense woods. I hold you,
as you held me, in an open hand.

Found Things

I stumble from room to room
lost like a young wild boy
whose pockets once were stuffed
with marbles and frogs,
foreign coins and knotted string,
a pocket knife and an empty
silver locket, but now has
discovered his clothing empty.

He searches under his bed, behind
bookcases, in the far back
reaches of his black closet
where he sometimes hides. Nothing.
Where could it all have gone?
Vanished as strangely and miraculously
as it all had come to him—
found things, gifts and thefts.

This has happened too often.
So this time before he takes
his papers and paints and throws
them to the floor, before he shouts
so that everyone in the distant
corners of his house come running,
this time he stops and imagines
a pile of lost things someone else

will find: unasked for treasures,
coins from places unheard of, string
from kites set free, an empty locket
once held close to a heart in love.
I wander the rooms of my house now,
not searching, not angry, not
even hopeful. I am merely ready
for the miracle of found things.

Endings

Sometimes the ending arrives without warning.
Somewhere in the middle of the second act
before the young man can speak what's in his heart,
offstage, the thick rope that holds the curtain
high and out of sight, loosens, unknots itself, rises
and snaps like a whip in the hands of giants.
The actor's words clot in his throat and the woman
never hears the phrase she so carefully rehearsed
listening to for the very first time. Perplexed, the
audience stands and steps into the street, wet and cold.

Another man wanders the entire night through a thick
wood in search of a trail. The moon hangs near
the horizon behind thick clouds. The story is an old one.
Thorns jabs the man's legs; green branches tear
at his face. We know the ending. At the darkest moment,
the man emerges from the woods and in his joy
and relief, he smiles and stumbles. Innocent of clear
passage, he walks too near the cliff and falls.

And sometimes an ending passes unnoticed.
The singer finishes his masterpiece and without pause,
not seeing the listener's tears, begins to sing
a new song, unpracticed, careless, contrived.
Or a teacher, remembering the ecstasy of his first lesson,
repeats himself, writing and erasing the same words.
Every eye turns toward the open door waiting
for the bell to ring for a second time.

And sometimes an ending is sweet. One night a father
hands his son the keys to the family car. One day
news of peace reaches the warden of a distant camp.
Slowly he walks down each long hall and turns the key
a hundred times. Early one morning, two lovers about to

scream across an unmade bed see into the other
and calmly smooth the sheets, still damp, still
fragrant, and turn to leave by separate doors.

Sometimes, no words. Sometimes, eyes open.
Sometimes, two hands held tightly loosen.

from
The Road Home

Voyager

It all ended when we bought a van. Yeah, that's what I said. A van. We'd been married for ten years. We had a seven-year old son. She hadn't worked in three years. I'd gotten soft and fat. My father's inheritance was running out, and she wanted a fucking van. A god damned Plymouth Voyager, to be specific. Seventeen thousand, three hundred, seventy-two dollars. And fifty-four cents. Cash.

I had already been beaten, you understand.

So we go out in the northwest part to town. The motor mile they call it. Out where the Shoney's is, the sushi bar, and the multiplexes. Out past the Smith and Hawken, the Pottery Barn, Banana Republic, REI, Barnes and Noble, Ann Taylor, Egg Head Software. Not quite to the new mall. And I wrote the check.

My wife thought she had finally arrived. A mother among mothers. Tooling around in her van. Hauling cupcakes. Not Pillsbury. But carrot cake cupcakes. With cream cheese icing. Maybe some lemon squares. Pints of Ben and Jerry's—Cherry Garcia, right? Pop a little Joan Osborne in the CD, and you get the picture. Maybe stop off for a cappuccino before the son's school lets out. Then the big event of the day. Stuff a half dozen kids in the new van. Pause a while, let the other moms check it out. *Hey...new van. Yeah, Plymouth voyager. It's so comfortable. And the kids, you know. I just love the juice holders. Show her, son.*

Then it all falls apart. Off to the waterparks. The pioneer farms. The canoe trips. All the parents in those shorts with a dozen snap pockets and Nature Conservancy t-shirts. And kids and their hundred-dollar Nikes and t-shirts Saving the Wolves. If I talk to one more person in a hipper than thou t-shirt, I'll fucking shoot myself. I'd rather hang out in a sports bar—with hockey fans.

Fuck it. It is was over. I didn't mean for it to end that way. But god damn. Who could listen to one more empty-headed, trend following, middle-class mom and dad discuss the philosophical import of *Forest Gump*? I couldn't god damn stand it anymore.

Searching the Parking Lot for a Poem

Though I've been silent several months,
I might now write about a man
and a woman in a parking lot.
This parking lot is very large,
acres, and there are but few cars
huddled beneath the scattered trees,
like cattle in western Kansas.

I would want to be clear, to make
understood that the distances
are vast, and that the air contains
a heat, something like four in the
afternoon, when the air is like
that last still moment inside
a balloon just before the balloon

blows up. I could say something
about the man and his marriage and
about the woman and her marriage,
but I might not. It would be better
to mention that his car was a
long way from her car but he walked
with her all the way to the far

end of the lot where her car stood
and then when she left he walked
all the way back. I would not make
the reader think this journey was
difficult, like desert fathers
searching thirstily for Christ.
I would just want to point out that

they were together for a long time
and then the man was without her
a long time. Merely that. Because
the poem is not about the parking
lot or all their walking about.
The poem occurs when they arrive
at her car and they stand looking

at each other. This is where really
huge distances are, the inches
separating two bodies. Here,
I find unbearable heat. Here
is the silence so full of words
they float between parked cars wanting
to call her back with this poem.

The Rose's Thorns

We do not know yet when rose's
leaves sharpened into thorns.
We imagine eons of abuse,
a million days of unwanted
tongues, the incessant nibbling
of beaks and teeth and hairy
leather lips hungry for a bit
of red, yellow, pink, or white.
For how many centuries
did the cedared breath of goats
part the tightly folded petals
to eat her sweet, sweet hips?

We do not know yet when rose's
leaves sharpened into thorns;
they might have hardened overnight
as tender hands that held her
pulled away to hold the lily
or the iris near. Might it have been
the shame of sunlight shining
on her face untouched by dew
or the ache of being pulled
apart to fall upon an empty bed,
the agony of scent unflared,
of flesh unwarmed in dark moon oil?

We do not know yet when rose's
leaves sharpened into thorns.
Perhaps she tired of weak perfumes,
the crystal vase, and poignant pose,

and urged herself toward wild.
I believe she wanted once to taste
a dancer's blood, hair aflight,
the guttural call, sweat run down her legs.
Their feet desire a hard dirt floor
to pound into. On his lip one
tear of blood appears. She finds
the pain that beauty can command.

290 West

So I'm driving down 290
west thinking what a day hot bright
dazzling I'm lucky s o b
saying to myself you ought to be
sitting beside me windows down
to hell with the a c today
imagining your beautiful
eyes looking at me little beads
of sweat along the curving line
of your gorgeous lips geez you're hot
I'm hot and I'm saying to myself
everybody's driving around
probably heading off to the pool
or the movies, maybe the mall,
just so it's cool and it's proper
and all I want to do is step
on it ease it into high take
you with me down 290 west

doesn't even occur to me
it's Thursday you dope these people
are working making cold calls or
picking kids up from mom's day out
doing chores getting stuff for home
this... even though I'm working too
just stepping out of the office
to buy you a little something
like a card with a poem on it
by someone who knows how to say
the things I'm feeling... finally
I realize they don't make cards
saying what I'm feeling at least

not at the Hallmark down the street
which is where I was aiming when
I stop in the heat remember
I'm you're married and no one's
cutting out on 290 west

today

Absolution

Come with me and step into this grove
of cedars. Let us breathe together
deeply scents of old forests mourning.
Let us spread upon these leaves bright quilts
patched by a thousand grandmothers, sad
gifts for daughters' daughters' beds of faith
and duty. If you wish I will call
paintbrush, firewheel and gay feather
to bloom again out of season or
I will drop blossoms of wild summer
roses into clay bowls filled with cool
water and with cloth torn from my shirt,
I will wash your hands and neck, your face
and feet, your breasts and sex. If you wish
I will sweeten your naked strength with
almond oil then leave you to rest in
warm cedar shade. I will stand beneath
the cruel sun until he falls from his
pulpit and the white moon sings from her
loft the song of your magnificence.
When you call, if you call, I'll return
to you. I will carry a bottle
of perfect wine, heavy on the tongue
with one last taste of cherry and loaves
of crusty bread, light as fish inside,
tasting of sesame and olives.
Together we will serve the other
who has always been traveling with us.
We who are wonderers all have our
stories but I, who love you now, hear
nothing to forgive. I can only stand
on firm ground and admire you. I see
volcanoes in your soul I hope some
day to dance inside. I bow before
the ten thousand births that nest in you.

"Hamlet"

I'm not thinking about the play,
but the poem that Pasternak wrote
for Zhivago, that Zhivago

wrote for Lara. Depending on
the translation, the poem begins
in confusion, or applause, or

turbulence, but we know something
has come to an end. We know the
poet is listening to echoes

of the past for some resounding
message from the future—for courage,
or wisdom, maybe even hope.

He stands alone talking to god,
himself, whoever, more or less
like I do now that you've decided

a life with me is not the life
for you. It's like some director
of community theater

had screwed up and scheduled two plays
on the same stage: you and I step
from our separate scripts into

a life not quite of our making,
but something at least our own, where
old words seem new, feeling someone

listened, not knowing where the action

ends. On one point, however, all
variations agree: Pharisees

rule the day—seems we can't avoid
untranslated terms translated
back to us. No matter where, when,

unforgiving order frightens
hungry desire with solitude.
The poem ends with a simple phrase:

"Life is not a walk through a field."
But lately I've strolled far from our
suburbs into wild rich meadows

full of songs of bees. The poppies
will shock you. I will wait awhile
if you should decide to join me.

Black Bowl with Apples on Old Tablecloth

I have placed a bowl of apples
in the center of the table,
an iron bowl, black and strong, its legs
curled under like snakes about to
strike. I have placed the bowl upon
a cotton tablecloth that my
sisters made sure was mine when our
mother died. It's white, with yellow
roses bordered by broad red stripes.
I've kept it all these years, I find,
so I could set a place for you—
the black bowl, yellow roses, red
stripes, apples the color of spring.
This time I will pick the fruit.

It will be crisp and cool and tart,
and with our sharpest knife, I will
sever skin from meat in perfect
empty circles, like rings, like mouths,
like the moan between your open
legs and we will eat this naked,
skinless fruit together, lips to
lips, teeth and tongue biting, chewing,
licking juices from mouth and fruit
and mouth not knowing which or who,
mingling, merging, urging into
the other, the three of us one,
you, me, and the promise of fruit,
all gifts of sisters and mothers.

Ark

When I lie beside you after making love,
I can feel the snakes in you have gone to sleep,
I slide my hands down their long backs
and hear them sigh,
I kiss their dreaming heads,
I nudge the tails, curved between your legs.

When I lie beside you after making love,
you lengthen yourself across the bed
and lean your back to me, you are as wet
and cool as a dolphin, and your breath,
deep and slow, is filled with the murmurs
of wolves returning home,
you lift your left hand and reaching
behind, you stroke my thigh
like five lizards licking the dew of communion.

When I lie beside you after making love,
and the clouds have opened and drenched
the bed, and the flowers on the nightstand
have exploded, dripping blossoms and wine
down the walls, and sheets and pillows
are clumped like debris in flooded creeks
and both of us lie shining like unearthed gold
at the foot of the avalanche,
I can still hear the echoes of a lion's call.

I want our bed to be the ark of our salvation.
I want to be the cave and plain and ocean
where the beasts in you are saved.

When I lie beside you after making love,
I listen to your hushed savannahs,
I do not know if it's dusk or dawn.
Something is resting, something awakes.

If You Should Ever Return

If you should ever return to me in the full light of your nakedness,
will I still be forced to hide my eyes in the hair between your legs
or will I stand, remote, unmoved, dumb in my dark room?
So many times, rather than be blinded by you, I closed my eyes
and bared my lips, tasting of your radiance, wetting the light.
My memories of you are of sound and touch, of taste and smell,
the sighs of salt rising from the seas, a skin that scents of silk,
a sweet fluttering riding the dust of our out-stretched wings.

My distant wondering breeze, the breath in me departs, quaking.
When I think someday I might see you, dull, unclothed, in a room
without shadows, the unillumined bed, I promise the last
lingering feathers of my tongue that I will lift the candles I prepare
for us and singe my eyes in bright sockets before the sight
of you displaces one memory of my blind probing into tangled rain.

The Way Things Go

It's always like this,
so why try to make it any different?

You're going to waste hours of your precious life,
maybe even days or years, looking for lost keys
that are right there on the carpet near the leg of that chair.

You are going to run out of gas
on that one night when you are out alone
driving down the dark road
out where no one ever goes,
except for that guy in the car way off in the distance,
one headlight burnt out, coming at you out of the black silence.

You are going to lose your job,
not just any job, but that perfect job,
the one that you had been angling for,
struggling toward, performing all sorts
of terrible, humiliating tasks for.
You know, running for coffee for people you hate,
taking heat for a supervisor's mistakes, staying late
even though you're missing dinner with the one you love.

And you just might have to go on
after that wonderful love packs her bags
and tells you that she won't put up with your shit anymore.
And you ask what shit? and she just slams the door.

It's just the way things go. Why complain?
Go on and accept that you'll survive this, too,
and sometime, often even, you will be happy.

Soulmates

You travel through your life with this other person
people have started calling by your name.

You allow him to walk in front
so he's the first person strangers meet.
How are you? they ask, and before you can answer
he's telling them something you've heard a hundred times
but never comes close to what you really feel.

You've begun to notice
that when you go out to eat he orders hideous, dangerous foods.
Sometimes he drinks too much and embarrasses you
with how he treats the waiters.
Then he grins and lets you pick up the check.

Still you remain silent.

Now he's making all your important decisions for you:
what job to take, whom to marry,
what car to drive, what part of town to move to.
He waves your paycheck at you as if he had done the work.
Do you remember the times he screamed at your children?

I'm beginning to wonder how long you'll let this go on?
What kind of death is he planning, do you think?

These are things I've been wanting to tell you

I don't give a shit about chipotle sauce.
I don't care where these peppers are grown
or special techniques best chefs use
to reduce heat and remove seeds,
to enhance that smoky flavor
so reminiscent of Indian fires,
which neither you nor I have ever smelled.

What I care about,
the only thing I've ever god damned cared about,
is the one tiny droplet of sienna cream
on the edge of your red lips, smiling.

And I only pretend to believe that Miller Lite is piss
and the only beer I'll ever drink again,
ever, ever in my entire life is some micro-brewed amber ale
made with Austrian hops and spring Canadian snowmelt,
produced only in limited quantities, but by some miracle
is available in Albertsons throughout the South.

But I told you the truth
when I said the butterfly
that paused, migrating North,
on the empty ice chest
three days after our spring party
made me see the unfolding joy of our life together.

And I couldn't give a flying fuck
about fabrics and furniture,
about what Martha Stewart or *Architectural Design*
would do with our space,
about how angels, or was it gargoyles, are in or out,
about how you want a room that John Tavener,

not Philip Glass, could settle into,
about how you just can't go to the Pottery Barn
now that they've opened a store in our Podunk town.

I just want to hear once more the Shaker tune
you hummed to yourself in sunlight,
holding from your garden a single rose,
wearing those stupid green plastic clogs
that you mail-ordered from Smith and Hawken.

An Animal Speaks of Speaking on Christmas Day

It happens every day, if you listen.
Somewhere, always, one of us is taken by talk.
We speak when we are moved.

We, too, were born cradled of two hands,
startled awake by pressing lips.
Inside us swirls the air that hums inside of you,
that breath that sang a lump of clay to be.

But that night was wild.
That night the dew of song fell upon us all.
We inhaled the music of a child
rocking in the arms of his own lullaby,
and we began to chant the holy pandemonium.
You could hear us everywhere,
rejoicing in the soil,
screaming in green distances,
prancing choirs of meekest speakers,
dumb beasts uttering with blessed tongues.

This is what I know.
Voice is vibration.
We do not choose to speak.
We are strings on a student's guitar
humming sympathetic harmonies when the master plays.
The goat skin of our souls resonates
rhythms from unknown valleys.
We inhale and are shaken until we pronounce
words keyed for our unlocking.

So, let me speak once more.
This year throughout your home
hang memories of turtles and snakes,
of cattle and deer; envision ants and ravens,

trout and wren, nesting in full view
in inconvenient places, on dining tables
where you want to place a candle,
on cushions of your favorite chairs,
in the pantry pushing oatmeal and grits
into dark corners behind beds of straw.

Let animals annunciate new wonders.

Then talk out loud yourself,
to the only one who listens.
Confess your desire
that winds inside your chest
should breeze witness to miracles.

Late Night

So a man drives around late at night
avoiding all the streets that lead home.
He knows lights are still on
that those who love him
are gathered round the table
talking, wondering what could have gone wrong.

They don't understand why it takes him
so long to return form simple chores.
He doesn't understand why
in spite of all the street signs,
in spite of all the maps scattered on the seat,
he would rather be lost.

Sometimes he even rolls down the windows
and lets maps fly;
he tosses out flashlights and matches
and says to himself,
Let's just see how fucked up things can get.

They know this is not the way things should be.
He knows this is not the way things should be.

But he hopes,
searching black streets alone
in the minutes closing on midnight
with gas running out,
he might find a second home
with those who know where he's been.

Angel of Santa Maria

An angel wakes
on Santa Maria Street
before sunrise,

stretches her light
in shapes like ancient signs,
like God's first words.
Her fingers rake
the world's wet soil
and tender rows sprout midair.
The turn of her
slender neck shocks song from the sleeping.

On one of god's
other avenues, he stirs,
facing the far wall,
listens for intonements
of dim dark dawn—

this could be the hour of panic

—but he feels a green mantra budding,
hears the light praying,
remembers dreams of an angel waking.

Setting Them Down

Wanting
to write
some poems
for you

I pace
about
the house

arms full
of sacks
brimming
with beautiful
surprises

unable
to find
clear space
to set
them down.

A Dream of Grace

In the morning, you get the news
your best friend has killed his wife
and you think, *Hey, that's a thing
I might someday like to try.*

We harvest wisdom wherever we can.
In rice fields, unnerved roads accept,
like fish, that floods will wash
them away. But it's never so easy,

is it? Floods, tornadoes, murder.
No matter how furiously we paint
onto old canvasses, something
of the abandoned work shows through.

More Metaphors
> "I'm a riddle in nine syllables." —Sylvia Plath

You're an oven baking sweetest breads,
a bank account with high interest,
a fat book with a gripping climax,
a water balloon hurling through still
autumn air toward the sleeping father.
O you dear double-wide mobile home,
you halt traffic on these narrow roads!
You're boxed fruit shipped to a cold climate.
I'm waiting at the station for you.

Laying on of Hands

So this is the way it happens. Somewhere around 3:00 a.m. in a bed not made for blood and screams, women hold the woman you love while you haul medical supplies, sterile implements, and oxygen tanks (just in case) from the midwife's warm Taurus in the driveway. All the while you're thinking, no, not now, in the morning maybe, the afternoon's better. You had everything planned: people to pray, a ceremony to honor the seven directions, something to beckon the deer and the wolf. And you were even wise enough to think of the elders. But, now, you forget to light the candles, and far away, the elders are sleeping, cheap paperbacks spread wide like curtains over their exhausted hearts. And the prayer people across town dream of a man falling, tumbling through howling clouds, toward seas heaving at the waning moon. It is at this hour that you return to yourself, and remember what you knew before you knew how to plan, before you began scheduling your epiphanies. It is at this hour that you remember that only empty hands can cup the light, that mercy visits only when the last appointment has ended. So when you are called—*If you're going catch this baby, you better do it now!*—there is no other way but to kneel since kneeling is demanded, to bow before the only heaven our body will ever know, to pull life, wet and frightened, into your palms and place him on the altar of his mother's breasts.

from
As Long as We Need

Midlife Christmas

This season he travels back roads,
admires frost-covered field stubble,
caroling lights on distant homes,
flicks off the chattering radio,

that insincere inquisition
of state affairs and high office.
He's abandoned freeways, the vans,
sports cars, and eighteen-wheeled commerce.

Yet his pickup is full of gifts.
Beside him sleeps his year-old son,
beside him, his mother, head resting
on the wings of the car seat. Soon

they'll arrive at home in the woods.
Tomorrow his son from the first
marriage returns. He'd not have dared,
two years ago, to have wished

for something as simple and true.
Sometimes night seemed never to end,
but one life has been made from two.
God gives us as long as we need.

Six Motets

1.
O you raveling thing who has no name,
you whom we have almost ruined,
mopping our pools of blood and piss,
cooling our brows in fevered night.
How can we return you to full furl?
How to cover our tables for bread and meats?
We dare not finger you for fear of threading you to dust.

2.
Our fathers were decorated shots.
They hung your name above their scopes
and built you hearths in the mobs' seared wounds.
Alleluja. Alleluja.

3.
Nameless One,
we call you all day long, each day long,
and pray for your abandonment.
Hosannas of horror. Horror of hosannas.
Our palm leaves swat your bloody brow.
We rip wings from angels' backs
and fire staggering miracles in magnified sight.
Hosannas of horror. Release yourself. Release.

4.
Refuse us our claim on you.
Forever hide your name.
Refuse us our claim on you.
Forever hide your name.

5.
Let us now murder on our own behalf,
cripple ourselves with tools of our own hands,
choke on usury of our own desire,

burn in landscapes of our own light,
brand with marks from our own coins,
rain dishonor upon our name, not yours.

6.
We will repent until pole ice melts.
We will cleanse in flooded plains.
We will forever ask your mercy.

Product Reliability

What weird energy machines we are.
Our children smile over cereal
and we introduce a whole new line
of compliments at work. We catch a few
lights green; then patience pours from us,
and we pause for lost Corollas crossing
lanes making their urgent and almost neglected turns.
A wife remembers an old affair;
her educated touch pulls her husband
into some still, grateful place.
He thinks it's the roses—
the ones she nagged him daily for
and he remembered at the grocery
while purchasing Bud Light and Salems.

But life is more than swipes of debit cards.
It's stranger, like autoimmune diseases.
Carcinomas pop up unnoticed.
Sometimes a family vacation is deposited
in a pale body in black shoes and six
months later reappears as a strip mall.
Two home runs on the high school team
rattle around in a teenager
and suddenly leave a girl crying
bruised and half naked beside the road.
Entire nations can go mad with grief,
invading indiscriminately, when one plain
enemy ruins a clear September morning.
How is that someone can eat the Bible
and spit on the poor? We are all one
paycheck away from oil drenched coast lines.

Listening and Knowing Where to Look

A shame in me says I'm reckless, says
I'm a banker with open vaults, because
I have these few acres out of the city
and do nothing with them, except do nothing.
Somehow, leaving well enough alone
betrays a dark contract that I was raised
to account to. So, I look around my friends'
yards and speak admiringly of the gas grill,
of the enriched rose mixture hauled in,
wheel-barrowed, and shoveled along
the privacy fence, of the cement curbing
from Lowes, and, oh, yes, the plastic
closet for the tools, politely placed
by the air conditioner behind the trellis.
When I do, my friends puff up proudly
like jays scattering sparrows at the feeder.

When friends visit me, they say nothing
of the leaves—post oak, live oak, cedar elm—
the layers of seasons banked against
the house, or of the height of the wild grass
or the shift in stalk color from copper
to gold. No one notices the difference
in how the cedar, dead two years, and
the cedar, dead four years, resist the wind.
If I mention this, their shoulders rise
and twitch as if a hawk had passed nearby.
They pat their back pockets instinctively,
knowing something is being taken from them.
Like I say, there's a shame in me that calls
me reckless. But that shame seldom drops in,
and I know not to listen when he speaks.

The Other Writers Block

1
A student stands in my doorway
confessing some desperate
blockage in my creative faculties
and before I can inquire
if she really talks like that
or if she picked it up, like Strep,
by listening too closely to exalted professors
at our *institution of higher learning*,
she tilts her head and does something
funny with her eyes and then
her lips, and says I wouldn't
understand, that nothing like that
could ever happen to me.

2
Remembering unfinished poems
from the beginning of the term,
I try to name once again
the stack of papers on the front
right corner of the desk,
I call it *a mountain,* then
dunghill. The phrase *a ringing
telephone I don't want to answer,*
runs through my head. Next
it's *a bouquet.* The pen scratches
on a piece of scrap *the tears
of black desire in a white sea,*
and crosses it out. Finally, I hear
*sprouting voices singing the irradiated
waltz in the polluted compost
of the twentieth century.* The hour
passed, I put away my pen and
amble to my morning composition
class, leaving the *metaphors*
ungraded and unremarked.

3
Even though it's my office hour,
I imagine that, if I shut
the door and stanch the flow
of words not my own, some trickle
from the reservoir of either hope or
memory might moisten the dry
arroyos of *my personal voice.*
The lessons, *write every day,*
write the things you care about,
write from your own perspective
begin to crowd the corridor and soon
one of them gets rowdy and rips
from the closed door my favorite
wry *New Yorker* cartoon.
Then all hell breaks loose and pretty
soon James Wright come barreling
in screaming, *I have wasted my life,*
and Rilke returns from the realm
of angles, whispering, *You must*
your life change. I begin
to envision myself an astronaut
or a penitent, anything cut off
and alone, a piece of string,
an insect husk. And just when I'm
about to yell they must silence
themselves and stand in line
like everything else, someone knocks,
and before I can ignore *him or her,*
a student opens the door and asks,
Have you graded my essay, yet?

Dark Night on Deck Upstairs

Every night I wake between one and four
to take a leak. The toilet is downstairs,
so I open the sliding door, step
on to the deck. Outside the city,
the stars stare down at me like cats' eyes.
My feet and ankles are stiff, but I try
to steady my legs, hold on to the railing
and stick myself between the vertical
slats and let it go. Maybe it's the beer
I drink to help me sleep, maybe my prostate
is beginning to warn me of my doom.
One night I heard perfectly how my dick
was this ancient part of me pouring
out a steam of memories in a language
I could not translate. I watched the arc
of wisdom—my kidneys and bladder sighing
with me—descend into the darkness, then
turned my eyes up to Ursa Major, the Pleiades.
Shaking myself, letting the last drips
fall, the sliding door closed tight,
I knew how easy it has always been
to vanish, to feed the roving hunger.
I closed my eyes, listened for silent paws,
breath, closing wings and open claws, listened
to the body's syntax, to the diction
of blood and nerves. The night was clear as ice.
The piss pooled briefly, then disappeared.

After Hades, Always Persephone
for my step-mother

Sometimes, I thought my father ruined her
like some force, wind or water, cutting
creases, ravines, into summer fields.
One moment, she laughed, lanky, two-pieced
in blue on the Mexican border,
tequila sunrise, poolside, held high,
like life cashed her in a winner.

Another, she guided the blind man
upstream to river's secret cavern.
Half-drunk on cocktails of disappointment
and duty, she changed his shitty sheets,
raged to him box scores, fed him pieces
of her impoverished heart. And I tallied
the income of his indifference.

Then for fifteen years, she bloomed again,
a crocus in winter, wisdom poured
from sober widowhood, grandchildren
blessed in pilgrimage to her temple.
Life claimed her and refused to let go.
After crows strip the corn and buzzards
glisten bone, what remains is courage.

Weekend Forecast
for Colleen

One day we will dine slowly and well,
just the two of us, talking about books,
remembering paintings from the afternoon
at the museum, remarking in passing
about what one of the children might have said
if he had walked one of the corridors with us
and had not caused a commotion and left us
embarrassed, apologetic, defeated.
We will share a little Pinot Noir,
but not so much I grow tiresome and dark.
There will be a hotel, not some traveler's court,
with a large room—tv hidden behind
latched oak doors—a deep tub and wide firm bed,
large windows, undraped, far above neon
and noise, where I will unrobe you for angels
to see. So please forgive me this year
if committees, contracts, sleet, and chicken pox
have made me a man who mumbles distant
promises about a quiet late lunch,
a slow drive beside the river back home,
azaleas pink and tangled upon the rise.

Dawning
for Theo

It begins really early. When they leap
into your arms, blue and slick and shiny,
panting like a sparrow. Or when they rise
and turn like a whale and your wife's belly
goes taut, and she calls to you, *Look, look!*
Or when you hear whosh, whosh, whosh, of radar
and nurses count heart beats and they're somewhere
between boy and girl, and you don't really
care to know for sure. Or, after the fifth
or twentieth try, when you know that this
time the heavens opened to your summons.

So, it doesn't surprise you those other
times later—when he stumbles through the room
yelling languages you've forgotten, when
he climbs upon the chairs and then upon
the table and stands proud like Sir Edmund
Hillary, when he grazes rubber balls
past your left ear, when he dances circles
to *As Time Goes By* til he plops backwards,
dizzy—that the heavens are still open,
that dawn never shifts into day, that light
always new, streaks golden upon this world.

Ice Storm

Ours wives don't love us any less than long ago,
just in different ways, like water become ice.
Where once there was a calm, wide river full of fish,
the silver of their affection still swims below.
Now we must cut circles through frost to capture them.
Think of it their way. We were once a blue sky, large
and clear and bright with promises of endless spring,
but we became thunder and rain, and then our dark
descended upon them cold and heavy with snow.

My mother would tell a story about a storm
in Illinois. The ice and snow began to fall
upon the winding two-lane. My father halted
to dress the chains in ungloved hands, jacking each back
tire, quickly adjusting links, while chill filled the car
and my mother quieted the girls in the back
seat, who had started their whimpering. *God damn,* it
was cold, but what was he to do? They weren't a mile
down the dangerous road before suddenly the chains
wrapped themselves around the axle with the roar
of bombers, land mines, and tommy guns. They hunkered
down on tins of sausage and saltines while strangers
in boots and warm coats repaired my father's mistakes.

It became the story she told office holiday
parties. The secretaries' eyes stilled in skillful
anticipation. Eggnog, laced with rum, lifted
to the fissures of their lips. My mother's voice
became more liquid each annual retelling.
My father filched a smile from some cold place along
the road that took him to his titles and gray suits.

A colleague tells me about her recent divorce.
The husband got the house, the good car, and left her

and the kids. Now his girlfriend, thin as fishing line,
has moved in. At night in the old bed, this latest
one spins dreams into the air she screamed and cried six
months ago. The colleague, who tended the laundry
of his stale career until their children were old
enough for school, is two months behind on her bills.
Her husband, always starched and dry cleaned, is filing
suit for her two sons. One happy hour after work,
I don't know why I took her there, I buy us both
a scotch, mine straight up, hers on the rocks. But I have
nothing to tell her. What am I supposed to tell her?

Mirror Stage

Near the end of the semester it all surfaces,
explanations, confessions. No matter how many
times you listen, the young will still surprise you.
They will admit outrageous amounts of alcohol,
personal pharmacological studies, unwise sexual
practices, addictions to bizarre acts of bodily
sensation. And then more quickly than they can down
a double shot of Jägermeister, they'll profess
an unreflective love for the Impressionists,
for Monet's *Water Lilies*, Degas' dancers at
the barre, or Manet's girl serving drinks at the Opera
House. One of them tells you his sister gave him
a Michael Jackson CD for Christmas and it changed
his life. Someone else says she owns all of Disney's
old cartoons, that *Snow White* is her favorite. Today
Jeremy confesses his love of Woody Allen's *Manhattan
Murder Mystery*. He brushes strings of hair
from his eyes, and I stare at a double row of healed
piercings bordering the feathers of his left eyebrow.
It's really cool, he says, *at the end with all those
mirrors in that old theater — everybody's cracked
up. You don't know what's a reflection, and what isn't.*

There was a night five years ago when my son might
have died, a man's two hands laced behind his neck,
thumbs pressuring the wind pipe, his last words almost
a scream, or a gurgle, or almost a growl. Now I visit
him in Chicago. He's in college. Before dinner,
we kill time in Myopic Books. I'm searching
for Richard Jones, Mary Kinzie, Reginald Gibbons—
where best to find abandoned books by poets than near
their homes, discarded copies by friends, fellow faculty,
and students, for whom purchase was sign of feigned
respect and affection. Will's off to psychology,
to Lacan, a college paper gone mad the way we teachers

hope an assignment becomes a project becomes
a vocation. By the time I make it to fiction, he's wandered
to philosophy, to Sartre. Finally, we settle at a table
upstairs near the big window opposite the other. I panic
here for the perfect metaphor—two planets in orbit,
parts of an atom, roaming canines, mosquitoes, lightning
bugs—something moving, something with gravity,
something occasionally bright. Father and son.

For a time, in the late afternoon gloam, we read
our separate books. I'm high in the air with the flag
pole sitter in Goyen's *Half a Look of Cain*;
Will's got *Being and Nothingness* pinned flat-spined
on the wooden table. Looking away, I gaze
out the window at the city, the darkness starting
to jell, the pedestrians quickening, students
with gigantic backpacks hunched over, a woman
with two bags of pillows, a man pausing at the door
of the Chinese takeout, a white bag in his fist
at his hips, and I see the city my son is beginning
to love more than home, a city my father was
denied because his mother would miss him too much
two hundred miles away. But he finally got away.

Before all this, as if on a scrim, is my son and
I sitting at a table, he reading, I looking away,
looking at, looking toward, whatever. His hair,
shaggy, wild, his sideburns, thick, tangled, his jaw
line strong. His nose is long like mine. Both hands
are flat on the table, elbows jutted out, shoulders
loom. His body lurks above the book as if he's
about to leap and take it into his teeth, wolf it down.
Then suddenly he straightens and stares at me. His lips
part, mouth opens. I find it in myself to still,
to wait. Then his shoulders drop, lips close, but his eyes,

softer, remain fixed. I don't know what he wants
from me, but I give him time to find it.

When I was fourteen my father and I visited
an old book shop in St. Louis. It was the centennial
years for the Civil War. He was tracking down
biographies of dead generals. How I found it
I can't remember, but I claimed an anthology
of British poetry and pleaded with him to buy
it for me. At home I wore the book out hunting
for a few poems that told me something of myself.
Then I found Blake's *Songs*. Slowly, the lights from
inside brighten on the glass and we fade. The neon
of tattoo shops, espresso bars, and a discount
cinema streaks the window with color. I ask,
can I buy you a book? He says, *sure, surprise me.*
On the way out, I take my copy of *The Blessing*.
For Will, I thumb Wallace's *Infinite Jest*, but decide
on Kundera, *The Book of Laughter and Forgetting*.

Burn Ban

Starting fires is easy. Keeping kids unkindled
is the trick. They'll stand close while you pour gas
upon the twigs and sticks. They'll inch their tennies
onto the jagged edges of wood and fuel until
you scream—before the strike, the pause for phosphorus
to catch, the daring but hesitant toss, and the infernal
roar—*move back, God damn it, do you want to die*!
This is the way it is with us now. Waiting for long rain
to soak everything through, the VFD to say OK.

There's always something to burn. Brush from clearings—
juniper is magnificently quick to rise red
and golden into the sky. Lumber scraps from new
porch and stairs, discards of structures well built, homeless
and unneeded in the hurried home economy.
Old school files—quizzes from 92's World Lit I,
Book 23 of the *Iliad*; from 95's Brit Lit II,
handouts on Shelley's death; 98's Am Lit II,
stories of Ellison and Faulkner; reports on
Patrick Phillips's poems from 05's Creative Writing—
struggling, almost shy, blue flames at tips of rising
corners, like fingers burning for the heat of ascension.

This week it was chickens. A door left unbolted
one careless morning, and in evening twenty-six
hens splattered and splotched across the garden
and yard by a fierce painter whose hands released
the dogs. The boys' favorite Golden Polish, Auntie Mame,
her unbusied body beneath cucumber vines. The white
Cochins, wisps of snow at their feet, left still as if
unpainted canvass near the hoses and the faucet,
at the fence of the playscape, a few feet from the new fig.
Big Bill, our one rooster, neck snapped, at the flapping

door of the hen house. Why is it important to imagine him
a hero, John Wayne swinging his musket at the Alamo?

The stench of burning feathers and searing meat hang
in the air while Jacob and I poke bones and flames
with rake and hoe. We do not talk. We watch the dead
disappear in evening quiet. The occasional ash feathers
into the air, riding the currents, red like the eyes in old
photographs: me, sixteen, four months after the chemicals
extinguished my mother and her cancer, fat cheeks
emptying onto the fires of a chocolate layer cake.

Or my father's cigarette brightening the night.
We are driving back from somewhere. It must be spring.
The windows are down. Again, he is telling me something
I should hate about myself. His right arm slashes
the air, while the left vices the cigarette and clenches
the wheel. Then wind pulls glowing embers across
the seat into my face, and I begin to slap myself, burning
and stinging myself. *Shit, Dad, Shit. Be careful. Be careful.*

The Upper Room

Imagine their dismay when office workers
and bureaucrats began showing up for lunch.
This was the place their prayers and savings
accounts had bought them—a small, clean, bright
kitchen beneath the highway, near the homeless
shelters, above the gay bar, beside the gallery
of angry ethnic art. They imagined word
would spread among the city's nomads. A good,
cheap sandwich. Thick, rich soup. A slice of pie,
the kind that grandma made for Sunday's family
meal. If you couldn't pay, they had faith God would
provide; meanwhile, what could they get you?
Do you know Jesus? Bill staggered in stinking of wine,
asking for paper dollars. They sat him down with a hot
roast beef and a few lines from *Revelation*. Once,
he returned, got the smoked Turkey, accepted *Timothy*
with apple pie, but they never saw him again.

That's the way it went for a while. Molly with her
two kids, long blonde hair like knotted yarn
and green stumps for teeth. She had kicked it,
she said, kicked it, and wouldn't start up again.
She stopped in three days straight. Molly wept
tears the size of pills every time they prayed
with her, then she disappeared. Benny, for
Benito, from Oaxaca, had lost his job processing
chickens in Giddings and was looking for anything,
anything. He got the vegetable beef soup, warm
white bread, and coffee. After he left, they couldn't
find the pecan pie they had baked that morning.
They wished him well, hoped that he would share.

Then slowly, as inevitable as winter, secretaries
in sensible shoes, state librarians with blouses

buttoned to the neck, filled the place. Nancy,
whose mother was in chemo, appreciated the smiles.
No, she didn't want to talk about John 14,
but could she get a slice of cherry to go? *Mother
loves your pie with milk*. Sharon's boyfriend
was on drugs. Larry was getting laid off. *Thanks
for listening*, both said. *No, I participate
in church*. They didn't know what to do with Erica.
You're good people, she said, trading recipes
for split pea soup. *I want my girlfriend, Angel,
to meet you. She'll inhale your chicken and rice.*
Wednesday nights, they wrestled with Acts. On Sundays
they sang *How Great Thou Art* and preached from Job.
They could not fathom why God's bright eyes had turned
so dark, why their fierce seeds fell to such poor soil.

Soon they planned to move away. Their last summer,
I lived out back in an upper room, a wandering
son afraid to return home once more in need.
I had degrees but no direction, heard a call,
but could not speak. Bussing tables three days a week,
I paid the rent and rode their generosity to the end
of the line and back again. Before she left—
twenty-six years ago—Marisa landed me her job
at the college among the Philistines and the sinners.
In my office on the second floor, through each
of God's seasons, I now listen to my students' tales,
their confessions and their lies. Jami's father suffers
gall stones. Leslie's boss won't let her off to take
a test. LaShanda doesn't know what to write on
essay three. I listen, and if I have something to suggest,
a book or poem, I offer it like an old family recipe.
I've known people who loved it, I say, *some who
haven't. If you don't, come back. I'll be here still.*

This Easter,

I will pray You
send the women
in to find me,

and I will be
gone, stripped down
to breath and dust,

witness to their joy
that all we fear
has disappeared

and what remains
is held by You
in mercy's light.

It is not that I

welcome disaster
like a slave
mid-passage
conjures the sea.

I accept each
generous day
as a child
grasps each

toy surprise
offered from low,
colorful drawers
at the dentists':

Colleen serving tea
in the morning,
each son, his
own particular

joy like a stamp
granting him
admission to
these wonders.

At night, we
gather around
the table, take
each other's

hands and bless
this meal, our
lives, You.
The candles,

we burn for
You at evening's
end to shadows.
So, in case You

didn't hear me
before, I am ready
when You are.
My family will

know where to
find me. They
will know I am
waiting for them,

waiting to offer
another grace.

Sometimes I cannot

look at photographs
of children drowned
in city parks
while parents worked

their second jobs.
I cannot stare
at TV news
of white-laced girls

raped by moms'
stoned boyfriends,
of a boy's broken
ribs and arms, healed

and hidden until
autopsy glare.
Forgive me. I've
wrapped myself,

frightened thing,
in this cold print,
to cry tonight
at your closed door.

Lord, remember

when Jacob—my
Jacob—was less
than two feet

long, he gazed
wondrously, deliriously
happy, it seemed,

as if he
remembered something
beneath the strands

of twinkling lights
we tacked to
the wall above

the changing table
no matter if
he lay there

alone after nursing
or with our hands
cleaning him,

soothing him. Lord,
this is what I
ask some night after

dinner when I step out
on the porch to
gaze at your stars.

Midnight,

faces from work
knotted
on a rope

cinched tight,
fisted
pen still beneath

crooked lamp
beam,
St. Matthew's Passion.

I could pray.

Such self-pity
must
make You sick.

*Was sol ich
denn
machen mit Jesu?*

What shall I do
with
my days?

Always

some faint shadow fleeing
from where I was looking

for You. Peripheral,

secret, a shimmering,
where space silently folds,

unfolds. Are You hiding,

or are there so many
prayers You must answer

that You remain in one

place so briefly You leave
only a trace for me

to know You have been near?

Fall in America

Why trouble yourself with closing your fist?
You make such a grand gesture of slicing
the open hand through the air and clamping

it upon the insect. You have to open
it sometime to remove the carcass
and broken wings. Often, I have seen you,

silent, astonished at what can disappear
from the tightest clinch. Are a job, a wife,
a vow, mere loose items released to wind?

You are still looking for the changeless rose
that caused first lost love to petrify mid-kiss,
a high school parking lot, the fourth quarter

unresolved, the quarterback's lonely girl taut,
pre-shiver in your considerate arms.
Memory is a blond hair, cum-stained and

pasted, in the back seat of your Mustang,
which you totaled the fall of your senior
year. Now you are puffed up like some success

plagued leper trading Ivy League diseases
in stock exchanges for the OCD set.
For once, admit to loss. Sell short. Wave.

Speed Limit

Think about the mosquito: four days
from egg to adult. What's the hurry?

Or there's a kid in Gaza praying
to God, strapping on his bus ticket

to paradise. What's he thinking, God
awards bonus points for those who first

rig the test? Some fragile incomplete
thing wants to be born. Some perfectly

strong, frustrated libido desires
divine fireworks or nothing at all.

We are but barges in this river,
wishing to be speed boats. Stuff rushes by:

insults, temptations, promises, cash,
and congratulations. It all gets

away from us, caught in fast currents
we're too slow and sluggish to employ.

The treadmill at the gym monitors
danger zones, tells you to slow it down.

The only lesson you've learned is you
could never keep up with everyone.

Warning signs are plentiful and clear.
What's with all this violent breathing?

Safe House

I know you feel unsafe, like a slotted
ceramic lamb in a room of addicts

out of their minds on meth. You listen
to their hands mumble something about choosing

another life, but their fingers grow claws,
bleed out an old hit about needs, stolen love,

fire and cinders. How can you remain calm
when you know your worth and glimpse the gleaming

hammer's head beside the ratty couch? There
is a child in a back room on the floor

in the corner behind the bed, clutching.
He has not forgotten you, but fears these men,

knows force and fatherhood, substance, texture
of abuse. One fear might be a forest,

keening. Another fear's a keyhole, framed,
distinct, focused on things you are seeking:

drug, hammer, or door. Did God place you here,
in the kitchen of hopeless revelry,

as punishment for your lazy devotion,
or on assignment to exercise the arts

that he taught you? You are filled with silver
and gold. This kid has dropped his dreams in you.

Uncollected Poems

Pedestal
R.E.L. at U.T.

> And I am spent with old wars and new sorrow.
> Donald Davidson. *Lee in the Mountains, 1865-1870.*

Most don't even notice me beneath these oaks.
They trudge past, weighted down by deadlines and backpacks,
hunched like soldiers shaped by burdens they bear for… what?
For honor? Glory? A parent's or professor's
praise? For wealth, greed? All that was mine, once, long ago.
But now I wait, immobile, paralyzed, like Grant
had me pinned in Petersburg. From this pedestal
tucked in shade between old Rainey and Calhoun Halls
I've seen it all, the calls to take me down, the pleas
to cut the present from its past, the tears, the shouts,
a face uplifted, stiffly proud, defiant, bold,
urging me, as at Appomattox, to fight on.
It's not my fight. I never wanted civil strife.

I did my duty. They forget the years I rode
in Texas, living on boiled meat and molasses,
battered by sun and wind and frontier loneliness,
a desert of dullness. Fort Mason, Camp Cooper,
Fort Chadbourne, Ringgold Barracks, Fort Brown, Fort Duncan,
San Antonio, Castroville, miles upon miles
on horseback, serving these United States, chasing
ghosts, Comanches and bandits. Honor as empty
as creek beds. No one celebrates men who do dull
work dutifully. I did not rank pedestals
back then. My sad letters home: *No grass for horses,
no shadows for men. What a blessed thing the children
are not here. They would be ruined.* As I was ruined.

One morning here, sun rose upon the old message
in a new phrase, *Black Lives Matter* quickly painted
on my granite stand, sprayed in flash attack like John

Brown at Harper's Ferry, another step toward
irrevocable break. They want to tear me down.
And now that Davis has been erased, a blank space
where memory stood, displayed in some stark museum,
I must concede, as I knew then, the poverty
of our cause. Slavery was our sin, and ours to find
redemption in. I could not command an army
against my kin, and so condemned myself to this
uplifted state of moral ambiguity.

Look at me. My sword is sheathed. I stare past you all
to a time before Sumter, before the Devil's
Choice. My feelings for my country were as *ardent*
and *unabated* as if still a green cadet
at West Point. Like Sam Houston, I knew what secession
would cost. Without slavery's curse, I would have faded
into obscurity, another minor blue
officer forgotten on frontier's blunted edge.
Coyote, cacti, and endless streams of idle
dreamers, speculators, like the little man who
commissioned me here. He could afford to resist,
outflank the inevitable revelation.

Robert Edward Lee reporting for duty, sir.
Around and above me these oaks sway. The autumn
wind from up the hill tussles a student's uncombed
hair. He remembers the holy promise that Truth
will set us free. He stares at me in shifting light,
verdigris, streaked in pollen, stained in grackle scat,
and ponders why I'm still here. I'm not a hero
for someone's lost cause. Take me down. Let truth march on.

Spring

Today the white startle against the sky:
Pear blossoms awaken my drive from home
to work. It's spring. I remember a well
an orchard of clouds, rain lilies, a stack
of branches gathered together, the flesh
of fall bundled for a late winter fire.

This cool morning, blossoms and blue fire
a random synapse, and that forgotten sky
resurfaces as real as the gripping flesh
on the steering wheel. My mind is a home,
today, for miracles received, God's stack
of small beauties tendered to keep us well.

But I can't tell you where I saw that well,
or orchard, or wood gathered for the fire,
or if. Was it from a book I now stack
in a corner for cheap resell, bought at sky
high collector's rates for show at home?
Or something seen and felt by and with my flesh?

It's spring. A dangerous time for the flesh.
We're all tempted to stare into the well
of memory, of losses, and fill home
with an emptiness that only fire
can cleanse. Desire and shame climb the sky
and fall back like debris from a smoke stack,

ash, snow, pear blossoms. Across town Joe Stack
decides to abandon the weight of flesh,
to point his Piper Cherokee into the sky
a full tank of gasoline pumped from his well
of hatred toward the unjust rich who fire
us little guys and send us packing home,

pink slips in pockets. And still at home
the letters and bills from the IRS stack
up in a chorus of accusation. *Fire!*
he shouts, *take my pound of flesh and sleep well.*
Then he tips his wings and falls from the sky.
It's spring. I am staring at the cool flesh

of pear blossoms; he sets fire to his home.
I remember a wide, blue sky. Joe Stack
ignites his flesh on impact and says farewell.

.

The Lure
after *Trebia* by Shawn Camp

The artist lays
a black line
so dark and thin
it is almost
invisible,
like a threat
unspoken.
On one side
it is water
or sky
leaping out
of itself,
arcing a gap
it somehow knows
is unfillable.
On the other
a field
or forest
overgrows
its edges,
attempts
to traverse
a darkness
it will sense
in memory
only,
a space
where roots
fail to hold.
It is a mark
with no
significants,
neither jar
nor fence,
nor empty
furious street
at dawn.

Scene from the Movie *Diva:*
And Maybe to You May Never More Return*
for Francine Taylor Davis

I guess it was in nineteen eighty-two.
Francine and I slouched low in our seats.
A darkened Varsity Theater, the arts
film house that became a bookstore, and now
sits empty: Time in real worlds does not slow.
Back then, we snacked on shared popcorn at late
showings and imagined the many fates
that awaited us, small town kids who know
they'll never return home. From the tenth row,
like children playing dress up, desperate
for a vision, the wizard's secret that
would make the future clear, we watched, true
believers in the image flickering
on the screen, the spoken word, and music.

For nearly thirty years, I've remembered
Diva and the opening sequence. Jules
enters a building. The camera pulls
up and away to reveal a theater
no longer grand. Its yellow stone stained, scarred.
from floor to balcony, the space is filled
with the hum of expected miracles.
The singer, draped in silver, stands center
stage, still until silence falls. When she turns
her head, the camera begins to school
us in art's possession, how it rules
both singer and listener. But a third
watches while the angel rounds her lips
and song is stolen by Jules' finger tips.

He is transfixed. Tears fall from the ocean
of his eyes as he rapes her song on reel
to reel. The diva opens herself, conceals
nothing, offers voice to oblivion.
Yet capitalists, the shades from Taiwan,

will purchase Jules' private tape, or steal
it. In this moment, Francine and I feel
something immeasurable, a love won
by ten thousand years of searching, human
wandering, forward motion, waves, the swell
of the divine pulled by heavenly wheels.
The aria ends, the story's begun.
almost thirty years, memory, a tape
on replay, a song I could not escape.

Always that one aria will stop me,
still me, halt me as if a ghost had touched
me, the hair on my neck rising, awed, clutched
by the haunt of what Housman called *poetry*,
but I feel it first as lost memory,
a weakened, pious echo of a church
bell heard somehow above the noisy surge
of day-to-day mechanics of money
making. It's our simple need for beauty.
Once, late, driving home, oppressed by work,
I punched KMFA, and drove the dark,
streets amongst the other lost, and Wally
was singing her farewell. I pulled over
and called Francine in LA, but missed her.

*"*E forse a te, non fara mai piu ritorno"*
From the aria *"Ebben! Ne andro lontana"*
La Wally, by Alfredo Catalani and Luigi Illica

Summer Returns to Texas

Summer is not your Yankee friend who comes to visit
once a year for a brief weekend of greasy enchiladas
and too many margaritas and dancing late at Stubb's,
the one who troubles your husband, that puts him
in that state about all the time he's had to spend with kids.
But he gets over it. He always does because sex is hotter
for a week or two, at least. You're sad to see her go,
late Monday morning, still hung over but laughing,
driving cautiously away in her Honda, windows down,
freshly showered blonde hair shining, except at the roots.
No, Summer is your cousin, the daughter of the drunk
uncle, who never really had a chance to grow up right.
She shows up in early spring. Her parents have thrown
her out, again, with no place else to go. You're her last
hope, her only choice. And you're so kind. She stands
in your perfect kitchen, the fridge door open, forking
leftovers from the Tupperware, wiping her hands
on her dirty t-shirt. Drinking beer. She says she'll get a job.
She says she'll help out. She says you won't regret it.
She won't stay long, not like last year when she upset
everyone at Thanksgiving. That was bad, she knows.

The Tab

Lee and Judy and I are riffing off each other,
sending various colleagues to one of Dante's
circles in Hell. *We know where I belong*, I say,
*let the winds swirl and the seas heave, I'll hang
with Helen, Cleopatra, and Francesca. Here's to love
and lust. May we never know the difference.* I grab
the lime wedge, salt my hand, raise my shot
of Hornitos, and touch their glasses lightly like a kiss
on chaste cheeks. Lee and Judy sip Mexican martinis.
Judy lets her lips drift down the rim as if in afterthought.

We are huddled around our usual table on the usual
third Thursday at Matt's El Rancho. Between us are
spinach quesadillas and a strange cheese concoction
that Judy always orders. It could clog the heart
sitting there congealing bowl just watching it.
Lee jabs it with a corn chip and swirls it clockwise.
The graceful wist of his fist shocks with its beauty.

I'm being good and refrain. During one of our first
dates, my astonished first wife commented that she never
had known anyone, before me, who drank tequila
in tumblers. I kissed her gently on the lips and handed
her the keys to the Volkswagen bus. We stopped
three times that night driving home before I could
unload myself of my enthusiasm. Judy and Lee
start up on the *psychopath from work*, their phrase.
We chatter about her every time we meet. They've
appointed her a chilly spot in the ninth ring.

This will go on a long time, so we order another
round, a double for me and a Corona chaser.
My sisters once persuaded me to steal two glasses
from the Cadillac Bar in Nuevo Laredo. They were
drinking age. I was sixteen and had a Sprite

or something. It was the first vacation since
our mother had died. We'd been to the bull fights
like always, and Dad wanted a tequila sour
like he used to drink with Mom when they made
these trips together. *Wait till no one's looking. Then
quickly slip them into the bag with the huaraches*,
my sisters instructed. Looking back . . .

There's a picture of Sharon and me and William
as a baby at Chuy's. On Friday nights after swimming
laps at Deep Eddy Pool, we used to eat there before
the Bush girls made it famous. The young couple,
their child, happy, relishing an incredible clean
feeling after swimming a mile in that cold water—
so many swimmers you'd have to do circles.
Then taco plates and frozen margaritas. Eight years
later, following a work party, I almost left
the place with another drunk married professor
from the department. It's a mistake I'm glad
I didn't make. Wonder what ring she's confined
to? *What goes around comes around*, Judy is saying,
still gossiping about the psychopath.

I bring up her daughter. She's tying the knot
to a nice guy from an old Austin family.
What did it cost? I ask about the diamond. Judy
rolls her eyes, hesitates, she's wanting to tell me,
but I shouldn't have asked. Then I remember
to talk about the tequila tasting William and I
attended last week at the UT Club. Pure agaves.
All Very fancy. Some had notes of vanilla.
Others hinted of ginger. Each coupled with
its own special *hors d'oeuvres. A hundred bucks
a bottle, can you believe that?* Lee asked me
my favorite. *I can't remember,* I say, *I am blessed
with indiscriminate tastes.* The waiter wanders by,
picks up plates and empties. He makes eye contact.
Another round?

Three Teslas

A red wing blackbird arrives in the back
yard like a star, like someone accustomed
to getting his way. He flashes the bars
on his sleeves, waits for others to ascend.
I'm listening to the Weather Report
album *I Sing the Body Electric.*

It's morning, the first Sunday in June. Three
weeks ago, tomorrow, I was plugged in,
a twelve-electrode lead for my stress test
EKG. Erik Gravatt's got a fast rat-
tat-tat rhythm going on the cymbals.
Zawinul lays some dark chords underneath

reminding us we are mortal. I think
of the days when Miles went electric, fused
sonatas to silence. Spring afternoons
at Schultz's, tall mounds of ground beef nachos
and pitchers of Lone Star, reading *Children
of Adam.* For me the heart's always been

a metaphor: *There all passions, desires,
reachings, aspirations.* One day, neon,
the flickering buzz of youth. Everything
I needed to know of light, I learned then
watching crest and trough of the waitress's
breasts swaying, the collar of her peasant

blouse gapped as she leaned in with another
round. Now it's Tesla's bony x-rayed hand
tracing nuclear specks through the vessels
of the chest. One room it's magnets clanking
above my heart. The next it's wires pasted,
stuck to soft tissue, dangling, measuring

the flawed lightning of my soul. *Keep walking,*
someone says. Tesla never loved a woman.
He never allowed the current of sex
to char the circuitry of his visions.
A crowd gathers. *Keep going. Almost there.*
Technicians. Physicians Assistants. *One*

More minute. Nurses. I am a broken
machine. Hands fall on me as the treadmill
slows. *Sit here. Get your breath. Do you have
Someone to call?* I have loved women. This
day, our bird feeder, hanging from the short
branch of the cedar elm, dips and rises,

riding silent waves, the weight of mourning
doves landing, leaving. Doves, the size of fists,
size of hearts with wings. A blood red sun has
risen above the trees. Docs warn that stents
remain intact only to three Teslas.
beyond that, exit wounds, metal slashing

me inside out, heart birthing, artery
freed and frantic, a backyard hose flopping.
This June morning, spray from garden sprinklers
prisms rainbows. A white dove grazes seeds
fallen upon unmown grass. While Shorter
shifts between screams and prayers, I'm standing

by the window sill sipping from my cup
of decaf. Blackbird struts but doves remain
unmoved. A long season still awaits us
before the fall. *Yes, I do have someone.*
I palm my cell and speed dial home. *It's me.
The test is done. There's been a change of plans.*

Mayberry Sequence
for my father

1
We love it even though we know it is fake
when the father and son happily stroll
the unpaved road. The boy stoops for a stone
to fling with mighty arm through a tree break
into the lake. This boy's simple delight,
morning with his father, fishing alone,
beside waters where light appears to float.
It won't matter if fish refuse to bite.
Wind whistles, and a voice begins to speak
like a trusted friend, *The Andy Griffith Show.*
It's the mid-eighties, my father and I
are casting for understanding off the dock
of nostalgia. Staring into the glow,
we sit together still into twilight.

2
We sit together still into twilight.
It's reruns now. It's all we watch, except
for when a game is on. I've made the trip
home for a long weekend. *Home* is not quite
what I mean. *Home* is where you wish to stay,
not where your father lives, where hurt is kept
boxed and closeted so it can't corrupt
the home you made when you moved away.
Ronald Reagan speaks of this, of the light
upon the hill, an image that Winthrop
preached ship board bound for Massachusetts Bay.
But I've returned to help out for a night
or two. Before adjusting the tv set,
I warm a meal and place it on his tray.

3
I warm a meal and place it on his tray,
Campbell's tomato, grilled cheese, Ritz crackers.
Um um good and *Good cracker, good cracker,*
corporate taglines I used to enjoy,
still form my Americana soundtrack.
Tonight it's lunch for dinner like Mother
would make when Dad, our weekend warrior,
went off soldiering, before cancer bivouacked
in her gut. The third episode today
showed Opie batching it with Andy, supper
ruined, a casserole cooked a crispy black.
Then there was laughter. That's how life's portrayed
in Mayberry—forgiveness each half hour.
There's nothing you can say you can't take back.

4
There's nothing I can say. He can't take back
three decades of insult and invective.
I will say nothing, and if not forgive,
I will refuse to remember the crock
of lies he fed me about my certain
failure. Back home, I have a son and wife.
It's reruns here of another family's life.
Opie cries out, *Do you love me again,*
Pa? Across America hearts ache
at Andy's rare cruelty. My dad will leave
the room, shut the door, pee, ignore the pain.
flush what makes it in, blow his nose, and hack
his lungs clear. Is this any way to live?
I wonder if he feels regret, or disdain.

5
I wonder if he feels regret, or disdain
for these simple folk and their dim country
charm. He'd left a town like Mayberry

back in Illinois, went off to Champaign
Urbana, got degreed, then Roosevelt
put him to work. A handsome guy, twenty-
five, money in his wallet, the floozies
called, *Hi, Doll.* Their dark voices could unbelt
a boy right there. It took will to refrain
and leave like Gomer, Barney, and Andy
eventually would. I know how he felt:
fear. Our futures lay beyond small town Main
Street. In America, we're all refugees.
You don't have to play the hand you were dealt.

6
You don't have to play the hand you were dealt,
just fold, reshuffle, maybe even call
a different game. At last resort, stall.
Why does Andy stay so long? Is it guilt?
What does he owe these fools, Goober, Ernest
T. Bass? Otis stinks of rot gut alcohol.
My dad asks for a beer. *Dad, you beat all,
you know that?* I say in my cheesiest
Andy accent. Why make things difficult?
The cancer's back. I grab him a cold tall
boy and gather the evening pills. *Arrest
me*—with four big swallows, his head will tilt
and he'll be out. I'll catch some Braves baseball
before waking Dad and getting him undressed.

7
Before waking Dad and getting him undressed,
I finish off the beer and make the evening's
call back home. *He's the same. We're doing
fine. Love you, too.* I tell my son he's blessed,
*Grandpa loves you. Soon, I'll make jail break
when Granny M returns*. The following
year, Dad was gone. We buried him, saluting,
where Mom was born, where love would overtake

him, what he called home. Twenty years have passed.
with another pair of sons, I'm still watching
Andy and Opie, hoping for their sake
they find a sweetness that can't be suppressed
or cancelled. Somewhere, someone's whistling:
we love it and refuse to call it fake.

The High Shelf
for Bill Henry

My friend, I have been pondering a point you made
about fame and the lack of it, about the shove
and push of mediated notoriety,
about your hopes, mine too, of taking a place
beside our heroes on the shelves of history.
You'll notice that my language here has turned a tad
old-fashioned. It is respect, a feeling close to love,
more than nostalgia, that invites a graceful
and tender tone when speaking to our youth's companion
about the faded phantoms of our once desire.
The thing we see today that shines was not a fad
that passing time or the latest trends can debase,
but late nights of cheap wine, conversation, and coffee
became decades of silence while we did the work
that God gave us to do. And then it was done,
or not done, like a meal we planned to share at end
of day, but had forgot to turn the oven on,
a life with so much stirring and so little fire.
And now you write about the simple lunch outside
beneath the oaks, a gentle breeze, and recommend
a book that makes an anxious heart accept its fate.
I read it late at night while children from my second
wife are sleeping. There's really nothing else that I'd
prefer to do than finish out the years we have
receiving word from you about the blessed life
you live with books. There's no time for regret. I'll save
the letters in a cardboard box my sons will find
someday up high as if it were a golden gift.

from
Last Work

from *Last Work*
    For Neal Adams

~~You think~~ y[Y]ou were looking for [~~strength~~] ~~iron~~   strength
God had something else in mind

Dissolving

Like [~~drinking~~] tea   sipping
Sugar [~~on lips~~]   viced ~~in teeth~~

~~A~~ t[T]humb smudg[~~ing~~]ed sweetness

~~Then~~ e[E]verything you desire [~~weakens~~] disintegrates

                 *   *   *   *   *

            moss and winecups
                skywater

                 *   *   *   *   *

He hears your cries
[~~He pulls~~] them ~~toward Him~~   Beckons

Winds ^ from hidden sources
  stirred

Hopes and miseries [~~cupped~~] away   scooped
[   ] Like dust   ~~Poured~~   [wind borne]

[~~Snapped~~] from   prayer [rugs]   Beaten
                            ~~the rug of~~

-
-

               *   *   *   *   *

[The Interruption]
~~The~~ window[thump]   ~~thump~~
-

                    beak
                 dream catching
                   ~~The~~ feathers

          [~~Dropping~~] crumpling, collapsing, descending
-

                        [~~grief~~]   ~~hope~~   awe
-
-

               *   *   *   *   *
-

Open
So much brilliance wishes to return

Don't make it wait
Until your flesh ~~dries and~~ wrinkles[, dries]

Joy lays siege
To your [~~pretended tenderness~~]   pretenderedness

Where is the gate where angels enter

               *   *   *   *   *

        bloodroot   beetsweetness
                algae receding/~~reseeding~~

* * * * *

Look up
The soul knows about rising
About choosing

About [the boxes] windows
We hope to [package ourselves in] frame ourselves within

Sunlight skitters

[The moment holds a ^ history
            [n entire]
Between two blinks of one eye]

Don't let the shadows and
Bodies [frighten] you   deter

* * * * *

    [evidence]   [substance]

* * * * *

the skin and its scars
tell their own story

            you can't cover [up] everything up
-
"It's not the crime, but the cover up"

from
Old Men on Tuesday Mornings

Old Men on Tuesday Mornings

Mostly, we talk about our fears, that we'll be forced to be
the kind of men that we would never wish to be. For me:

it's the guy scooting about that motored thing at Safeway,
because my knees and gimpy hip can't bear the weight of my

bad habits. Thank God, I'm still limping along, leaning over
my cart, pushing past the Werther's caramels, the Ensure,

and Depend. Who knows how much time I have before I give
up and become that creepy coot, basket brimmed with lottery

tickets, cheap beer, cheese, and condoms! The last merely for show,
we suppose. Even now, before that dreadful day, we know

that women, including wives, have begun to indicate
disinterest in any dis-ease we could communicate.

Then there is work. Because pay checks have shrunk (like the other
parts), one of us worries his lucrative career will come

full circle, forcing him to take, again, the measly job
he jettisoned so proudly when the gravity of youth

gave way and he entered the orbit of adult success.
What will become of us, we fret, now that our contact lists,

like our backs, have begun to weaken? Which will give out first,
our pensions or our pride? But we laugh. Our fears, unruly

pets, are locked away in kennels of possible
futures. We take them out for walks and water breaks. Perhaps

a shit. Our conversations are plastic bags we pick up
worries with. So we keep talking. Hey, we've survived this long.

Ode American

> "It were a vain endeavor,
> Though I should gaze for ever
> On that green light that lingers in the west.
> I may not hope from outward forms to win
> The passion and the life, whose fountains are within."
> --Samuel Taylor Coleridge

1
A poet walks into a coffee shop
and realizes right away it sounds
just like the opening line of a joke.
Slightly chagrined he orders a double
Americano and warmed blueberry
bran muffin. The cashier with long black beard
smirks at grumpy old man with short gray beard
as if he knew something about time and
happiness the old man had forgotten.
The poet frowns because he knows tempus
fugits no matter how many diems
one carpes at the latest hipster bar,
but he will merely prove the barista's
expression by making the obvious
point: been there, done that. Finding a table
in slanted light, the poet carefully
arranges his moleskin book and fountain pen,
exhales as if to clear a century's
decline from his uncollected conscious,
and promptly decapitates the muffin,
whose scratchy ingredients will ensure
a flow, if not inspirational, then
at least guttural. Haplessly, he waits.

2
And waits. There is nothing to say except
today is like another day. The new
refuses to undo the tedious
repetition of his somnambulant

expectations. How can he wake himself
each duly pleasant morning to the crack
of joy? Comfort is so habitual.
In his psyche's Ipod®, the greatest hits
of his life's soundtrack is set on replay.
A poet walks into a coffee shop.

3
This morning, the bussed and sparkling tables
are burdened with optimism's debris,
push cards, coyly placed in jaunty angles,
attracting maximum accidental
interest from the consumer's practiced
disinterest. Twelve thumbnailed Photoshopped®
headshots aimed at our un-self-reflexive
recognition of individual
inadequacy. Inspire and Improve:
two days, twelve workshops. $500.
Each face beams satisfaction, grins brightly
the unkept secret of success. Sell, sell,
sell yourself. No matter the crisis or
the cause, the product of the Conference Class
is hope, hope you, too, can be a leader
possessed by confidence, initiate
member of the meritocracy of poise.
Happiness spreads from your uncritical
acceptance that aggrandizement becomes
the How-To Masters, the Fix-It Prophets.

4
Fork over a Franklin for fresh caffeine
and roughage, account for change, before
dropping a Washington into the jar.
Another morning gazing at passing
suits and heels, power's dress code paraded
on downtown sidewalk runways, these models
of success posing in perpetual
motion, machines bilking by the quarter

hour, each step scheduled in some inner
daily planner. The poet watches these
name-brand lives pass before his generic
eyes and dies a little himself before
recalling Poor Richard's thirteen values.
jots notes to remember frugality,
justice, moderation, tranquility.

5
The poet's mind escapes to a nearby
park. Between bitter sips, he roves, eyeing
the hopeful: mothers guiding strollers pray
for ancient knowledge women now-a-days lack;
the homeless wish for one day without cops'
batons; the old woman, bowed by years like
a harp, hums a tune that sounds like Gershwin,
while she dances her walker from shadow
to sunlight; a vet with a blown left arm
balances on one leg and breathes into
his meditation. Enlarge, Enlarge, don't
Blink: the dry stream, where the homeless sleep,
watered settler's horses; the oaks' massive
branches shading Apaches roasting autumn
acorns. Deer, bobcat, fox. Migrating monarch
butterflies, cedar waxwings, golden cheek
warblers. Great Sea receding, arriving.
salamanders, oysters, mussels, algae.
Today, the mockingbird cascades his joy,
pouring over everyone in the park,
drenching us in celebration. We should
be prancing, like children, through the sprinklers
of song, dripping joy's generosity.

6
Then three or four Iphones® erupt across
the cushioned complacency of the mock
living room. Ringtones and alarm bells assault
the cheerful harmonies, corporately

condoned, caustic warnings of impotent
dangers: Amber's stolen children, wayward
seniors, timbers blazing, creek beds raging,
rapture's raising. The gray professional
a table over mouths politely toward
the poet's fluster, another shooting.
Our daily dose of penance, a nation's
tithe for the freedom to protect itself
from itself: possess more guns because we
own too many guns; kill because we fear
we will be killed. Work and idle moments
cease while faces screen themselves in horror's
daily pageant. Mournful anxiety
drowns out the peppy hit parade until
it morphs into paranoid sympathy;
and soon all that is abnormal resolves
as empathetic congratulation.
We dodged another one. Now, where were we?

7
Two doors down from the coffee shop, a man
crouches, knees to chest, folded like a closed
pocketknife. His downcast face rises, glints
like a bade opening as the poet
approaches, but turns toward the suited man,
shining and fit, gripping his large To-Go
in one hand, folded bills in the other
extended casually between two
fingers as if tipping the concierge.
The poet jumps to grab the still open
door, ponders why he feels he's just been cut.

8
It's pledge week on the public radio
station the coffee shop pleasures patrons
with: cough up dollars for news you can muse
to, classical tunes that you can brew,
Dude. For four double Americanos

a month, the poet — he is reminded —
can be membered as sustaining freedom
of thought, liberal arts, the good life, hope,
the philanthropic way. The cultural/
social stock exchange at play, Carnegie
for middle-brow stiffs. Survival shifting
shapes as Maslow may. Music marketed
as meditation, art advertised as
happiness (like visual cocktails, booze
for ocularly abused), poetry
promoted as self-improvement (metered
mysticism for misanthropes). Today
the pledge drive starts. Do your part, the poet
pleads, abandon commerce, return to art.

9
The poet plugs into his own playlist,
that personal mix of philosophical
admonitions, essential memories,
and meek reminders of beauty's dues.
Old man, beware of darkness, may you stay
forever young and love one another
right now. Today it's old tunes heading down
to crossroads, laying down sword and shield,
catching trains to Macon, singing farewell
to Baby. Patton's watching water rise
and says he'll drive her to the edge of town.
Mississippi John's got the coffee blues,
goes all the way to Memphis to bring his
lovin' spoonful home. Nodding in mono,
the poet bleaks his morning by wearing
other people's blues. Blind Willie McTell
knows when a white man go to the river,
take him a seat and sit down, the blues overtake
him, he jump and drown. Not me, the poet

croons. His only trouble is that he has
no trouble. Lord, have mercy, he reflects,
everything, even grief, is delusion.

10
One chilled morning, the town is filled with fog
so dense that past and memory captains
the car. As if a character from Twain,
the poet steers the route his knowledge maps
in imagination, expectation
read and tallied through numbers and colors.
Three streets and right. White headlights blaze passing,
like barges. Avoid. Safe passage tethered
to taillights, like Alaskan prospectors
in London, stepping into each other's
prints. Anticipating the coffee shop's
green sign through mists as if marking a wharf,
a dock, a clean, bright place to contemplate
how present and past splash against the banks
of the future. He drives ahead with hope
faint, coffee with cream, Americano
Dream, another AirMac® seeking freedom.
Time measured, not in minutes nor hours,
but in refills and language beating toward
the bottom of the page. The poet sips,
declaring his independence, and writes
A poet walks into a coffee shop
and sits alone. Then waits and turns within.

Little Storm

I won't forget you, Little Storm.
What do we become if one
by one the memory stones that line
the path behind us disappear?
We turn around and gaze
upon the open field, the river
carrying everything away, and
in the distance a grove of aspens
quivering in the cool late afternoon
breeze, beautiful, but we are lost,
drenched and not knowing how.

Arroyo Sunset

Evenings, the two sat on the porch
watching the disappearance of time.
One knew more than the other
the darkness that rises inside,
then rushes forth, uncontrolled,
like May floods in a dry land,
the roar and debris bursting
beyond the banks of otherwise
peaceful and gentle waters.
One wished to rise and walk
out past the fence line, just to see.
The other held out a hand,
Let's just look from here this night.

Deep End

I want to write a poem about my father, but
my language filter's clogged. As I've become my own
Old Man, I realize that it has been decades since
I have tried to please him. Sure, I was one of those
kids who preened at the edge of a diving board,
the summer sun staining me like a berry, *Look, Dad,
look at me*. But when I had emerged from the splash,
he had already walked away. He has been dead
nearly half my life, and longer still since I hoped
that he would turn and, seeing, drench us in light.
This is why I want to write the poem, because,
last night, in a dream, as I baked in the lifeguard
stand, I saw him waving in the deep end, drowning,
and I woke before deciding what to do.

Heirlooms

When they were younger, the husband
could not understand why his wife,
whom he had married for hidden

skills and absent inhibitions,
always insisted on pruning
the wild, rangy heirloom roses

he'd shamelessly planted along
the front walk as his personal,
yet private, congratulations

that his house, more than his neighbors',
was where extravagant beauty bloomed.
His wife cut them short, almost flat

to the ground. She had her reasons,
which he had never understood.
They grew back wilder and fiercer

she said. The same applied to hair,
but she never cut hers that short,
except once, that last time, years ago.

I see that old man now each spring
out front clearing up the tangle,
cutting back all his knotty trunks

to the ground. He has his reasons.
And we neighbors luxuriate
in his tidy extravagance.

Open Carry

You don't want to stare
but your eyes keep slicing his way.
Then your raised chin aims
your buddies' attention to the guy
at the counter and the weapon
holstered against his lumbars.
You weren't afraid, but now
your body begins somehow
to nudge you from the inside.
Never have you feared of terrorists
or desperate seekers of oxy or meth
in this second Tuesday's La Madeleine
until this cowboy entered.
Stirring your black bitter
with a couple of regular Joes,
now the hackles spike as if you were
a pack of dogs lazing about the yard
licking and scratching
and shooting merely the breeze
when suddenly a wolf saunters in
all strut and insult to your canine sloth.
Your ironic smile about an article
in the Times or something Brzezinski
and Scarborough implied this morning
about Trump begins to arch
into a snarl and an unpracticed growl
rumbles deep inside your chest.
Another white guy with a gun.
The cartridges of memory spin
until you see yourself through
the sights of some old western,
meek farmer come to town
to swap stories and trade for sundries
the wife has been wishing for.
But the vigilantes are thirsty

for revenge, whenever any is called for.
So you apologize to your friends,
say today you need to get home early.
Still you decide to carry proudly, openly,
for the dark stranger to see, your box
of rich surprises with its pink bow,
your butter croissant and Sacher torte parfait.

From What Planet
for Colleen

She stands in front of the granite counter
in the kitchen, a knife clasped in her right
hand, the carrots, celery, sweet onion,
hardneck garlic separating, falling
apart at her quick focus. Sunlight wraps
around her from the high windows above,
her strong shoulders still during her cutting,
her back straight and bright. When she turns to smile
at me, the glare of love almost blinds me,
stumbles me backwards into another
room. We have loved each other for nearly
twenty years. Still some days it's as if she
just landed in my life, this familiar
stranger, this alien inspiration.

Small Bird

I'm slow to recognize the urgent language
of small birds. One morning, sitting at a picnic table
under shadows of El Capitan in West Texas
reading Thomas Merton, I finally awoke
to chirps, gurgles, and squawks of songbirds
in low brush nearby. How long had they
been screeching? My awareness gradually unwound
from distant cathedrals and returned to high desert.
I have lost my notes from that day, so I can't
identify the memory birds—Mountain Chickadee,
Bewick's Wren, Virginia's Warbler?—but they were
a noisy bunch as they hopped and leaped among branches
and spikey leaves. Then as they quieted, it emerged,
the Black-Tailed Rattlesnake, their danger now
open where every creature could see. This afternoon,
I eased from Jim Harrison's songs to small gods,
to the racket of jays and warblers in the oak
of my neighbor's yard. My old lesson sluggishly
slithered out of the thickets. Searching for trouble,
I found it twenty-feet up—the buff-breast
of a magnificent hawk. Even from my distance, feathers
so soft, they looked like fur of a beloved pet.
Tiny birds jumped and fluttered, yelled and shouted,
reminding me of a scene in a movie maybe
I have only imagined. Peaceful citizens, mothers,
shopkeepers, gathering around a lone man
sitting on a park bench, pointing, crying,
Him, him, beware, that's the man who did
those awful things! Making right, assigning shame,
a community surviving in its wisdom.
I always wanted to know what a hawk knows.
Today, I watched him uncoil and fly away.

Ghost Story

I told her I didn't believe in ghosts,
and there she went, fading into evening
lifting those pale fingers in half a wave,
a smile like she had just denied a kiss.

And how are we supposed to carry on
through this life that seems so like an open
plain obscured by sharp shrubs and swirling dust?
We watch for water, vultures, a barbed-wire

fence, but the mountains rise in the distance
always a couple more day's ride away.
We old men gather at a campfire, where
that last wild part of us can warm itself.

Our good companion, who is as lonely
and lost as we are, tells us a story
about the wife who loved him more than money.
He says he sometimes sees her ghost out here

when moonlight lies beside him and nudges
him awake. I nod as if I too believed.

Bio

You walk into a room and stop
because you can't remember why
you went there. Are you lost or are
you where you always planned to be?

No one blames the rangy pumpkin
vine for its wild, unruly life.
One day a seed breaks open. Greeny
desire squirms through darkness toward

the light. Hope—or is it something
violent like anger, greed, fate—
forces itself into and through
a crack, an ache, an imperfection.

Some God pours someone else's shit
upon you, and you find a way
to discover the good in it.
The vine grows where it can. The sun

changes its place far, far away,
all day, every single day,
yet the vine never stops. It roots
for a time, and moves on. Then all

these beautiful blossoms emerge,
delicate things. Look what happens
to them. They morph into tough nubs,
ugly fleshy failures, while you

keep urging ahead unaware
that behind you those shameful

false starts have grown large, succulent,
the objects of celebration.

Wherever you go, it's a new
room. You ask yourself "where am I?"
All you know is where you've been,
and all the effort left behind.

from
2018:
Found Poems and Weather Reports

January 23

I suppose it is good
that our lives
are not like lizard's tails
and when some god
has yanked at us too hard
and ripped off
a few years
maybe if we are patient
slowly
those years come back to us
green and hopeful
maybe different from before
but maybe not
who knows
because
we would begin to think
when will this end
does this adventure
ever wrap
well it does
eventually
Nicanor Parra
has finally died
that's proof

February 14

Valentine's Day
Ash Wednesday
today
love day
and
ash day
repent day
ashes to ashes day
kiss me my love day
I love you forever day
I am a sinner day
17 dead in Florida day
another white kid
angry at his high school
armed with an AR-15
4th school shooting this year
this year this year
and the Republicans
are running around with their
prayers and condolences
tucked into collective asses
CYA day

April 22

Mahler's 2nd
at JMU
with its orchestra
and chorus
and orchestra and chorus
of the Governor's School for Arts
just college and high school kids
and their teachers
what an ordeal this symphony is
to listen to it
is to churn in sentimentality
dread chaos hope anxiety
unfulfilled searching sighs
and growls never ending tumult
yearning joy timpani harp
trombone oboe cello and voice
rise again yes rise again
and again and again
and fall and fall
and rise again
in our greatest pain angels
turn away but we will rise
find our own wings
we will find our home
in the universe
we will rest in the light
of a never-ending dawn
the ovation stands and
a sweet pimple blotched
girl with stringy blonde hair
presses her violin to her chest
tears soaking her smile
a joy and the ever-present
sometimes misplaced
gift

May 3

Standing at the second-story
window looking east
the sun hinting behind
the neighboring houses
I yearn again to be awed
inhabited
the film of my humanity
cleaned wiped away
so that Your light
can pierce me
to the kernel
and burst outward
so that I see
with Your illumination
imbued
with Your charity
these trembling leaves
spring greened
in unexplainable hope

I am owned
down to my nuclei
by doubt

June 21

A two-year old
in red sneakers
sobs
as her mother
is searched
near the banks
of the great river
they have been traveling
for a month
from Honduras
escaping gang violence
an unknown risk
thought lesser
than the known

A five-year old girl
cries begs
to call her aunt
the number
a memory
a hope
a lifeline

A toddler
crawls on a colorful
alphabet rug
A for Alligator
L for Lion
O for Owl
N for Nutria
E for Elephant

Headless supervisors
in shoes covered
in disposable booties

hundreds of boys
fenced caged kenneled
in remodeled box stores/
stored like overstock
muraled presidents
watching silently

The question on everyone's lips
        where are
        the older girls
and Trump pretends
to undo
what he pretends
he never did

The border guards
ask the mother
to strip the laces
from her daughter's shoes

Another child weeps
        Papa Papa
        Papa

July 24

Li Po tells me
I should be
drinking
that's a happy thought
maybe I should
flee the house
maybe I should
take a walk
beyond the milk spills
of city lights
maybe I should
listen to the moon
sing to me
of broken urns
dipped into cool rivers
and lifted out
dripping
already half empty
maybe I should
stumble
into a stranger's yard
fall on my back
let hours of dew
soak me through
and through
and simply listen
to the voices
of someone else's house

September 16

My girlfriend
in high school
sat behind me
last night
in a dream
she is a beautiful
woman
now
still
with eyes
like those
of a wise wild animal
like a mare
still sleek and strong
she laid her hand
on my shoulder
leaned toward me
nuzzled my neck
and whispered
I am lonely
suddenly
I woke
shaken
and before
I could open
my eyes
I spoke
into morning
toward imaginary
unfenced fields
I know

October 24

So on Facebook
all my poet friends
are mourning
the death
of Tony Hoagland
at 64
ha I think
I outlived him
ha I think
now we know
that irony
does not prevent
or cure
cancer

They add hearts
meaning "love"
and faces with tears
meaning "sadness"
and thumbs up
meaning "like"
that one confuses
even me

But ha
I think
maybe now
I will be able
to write a poem
better than he
wrote
has written
is done writing
at least he won't
write any more
poems

better than
my poems

Then ha I think
I am still getting
the whole thing
wrong
every photo
I see
of Tony Hoagland
shows him
smiling
like big broad
shit eating grins
damn I think
good job
Tony

November 18

I live
2697 miles
from Paradise
California
Google tells me
I am
1 day and 15 hours
away
if I drive without stopping
if I did
when I arrived
I would not find
Paradise
unless one thinks
Paradise
is 14,000 burned out houses
instead I watch
the videos on YouTube
of the Camp Fire
and of the Woolsey Fire
North of Malibu
parents singing
to their children
and the walls of flame
stretching out
fingers of fire
blazing stalks spitting embers
crimson teeth
caught in the currents
and the child begging
are we going to die
the parent maybe making
one last lie
every promise
is a prayer

how can it be
a traffic jam leaving
Paradise
automobiles stalled
and abandoned
a neighbor frantic
breathless sprinting
through the midnight
dark smoke of that terrible
morning
and
there I was
last night
in the auditorium at EMU
watching listening
to students
in their end
of semester gala
playing Bernstein Merchant
Holsinger Mussorgsky
and concluding
with Faure's Requiem
and that is why
I woke up thinking
about Paradise
    Requiem aeternam….
    Kyrie eleison
    Christe eleison
over seventy have died
and maybe a thousand missing
    Free the souls
    of the dead
    from the punishment
    of hell
    and the deep pit…

    …into paradise
    may angels draw them
    on your arrival
    may the martyrs receive
    you and lead you into the holy city

New Poems

Symptomatic
images from the film *The Assistant*

The car outside idles. The chilled, dark hour
before dawn. The place where duty waits

for you to flick on first light slumbers
uneasily in its own fierce, frantic silence.

Someone will always count the minutes
that you are late, the hours their questions

languished unanswered. In this morning's shower
you fingered the flesh where fear and shame

have stabbed. The empty streets will hiss, traffic
ambers glisten their blinking admonitions, but

someone important announced he needs you back;
so it's a calling, or, at least, you were called.

Though no one's left to straighten your tie, hurry,
or the neighbor's dog will wake and snarl.

The Age of Misgiving
two images from the film *Song to Song*

Think about the ocean, the shore,
waves collapsing in exhaustion,
then the clawing, the reaching,
toward no hand stretched in the sand
until they thin into foam, into mist.

And think about the rope, knotted
around your waist, the tugging,
the pulling. You are caught, like a fish.
Someone else grips the lead. What is
next? The net, or maybe more water?

Or is there no ocean, no rope?
Yet desire keeps spilling out of you,
and you cannot resist giving yourself away.

Ambition
after "Rumpelstiltskin"

Once upon a time,
we are all imprisoned.

Once upon a time,
we all slave for the king.

Once upon a time,
we all bargain away

our parents' dearest gifts
so that we can merely survive.

Once upon a time,
we all spin the lightest gold.

Once upon a time,
we all offer our children

to some dark stranger.
Once upon a time,

we all have to name
that awful thing inside

that fulfills our wildest dreams.

The Dream

I once dreamed of wedding a witch,
of holding her warty hand in mine,
clutching her sharp and pungent hips
close, and warming her icy lips.

The fairy tale promised a happy end
for both of us. My love would water
the parched seeds of her voluptuous soul,
and I would die, delirious, in her spell.

Lists

I keep thinking that I missed something,
somewhere, sometime, way back whenever.

Maybe it was that kid with the pamphlets
in sweat-soaked shirt shuffling his scuffed

Tom McAn's on my front porch. Maybe it was
the meeting I skipped with the career counselor,

so I could toss a frisbee with that girl
whose name I have forgotten and whom I never

had the courage to ask on a date. Maybe it was
deciding not to return to my small hometown

for that job that I thought would kill my soul.
Maybe it was the endless lists I made,

things to do, books to read, beers to drink,
people to meet, projects, hobbies, jobs,

you know, making the lists, just making lists.

Knot
        after an image by Jericho Brown

Sometimes, I feel like tying
a bow around my tongue

so I will remember
not to talk so much.

Algorithm

The old gray guy in the shack
behind the house likes to think
he is done with poetry. Then
a neighbor shouts over his fence

something about end times,
something about parents with guns,
something about babies without
the right formula to unlock the cage

of compassion—governmental
or corporate or theological.
The leaves tumble to the earth
like bricks, cluttering playgrounds

into ruins. Everything is crashing.
There are just too many nouns
to account for, and so few verbs
that speak for mending.

SOS

Someone reported the bodies
piled in the freezer
at the old folks' home,

and a mayor was fined
for violating his own city's
stay in place order

to purchase a six-pack
of chilled imported beer
at the convenience store.

We are all finding it hard
to live with ourselves.
Like vampires, we avoid daylight

and mirrors. I don't know
how many nights I can hide
from Netflix. Where I live

winter has not released its grip,
and each morning I struggle
to pull back each finger

from around my throat.
I am hoarding something
and I don't know what it is.

Come, come quickly, I am
reporting myself, now, before
there's a crime I cannot explain.

Mirror

Someone's leaving dishes in the sink
and refusing to wash them. Someone's

letting newspapers smother the kitchen
table. There's dirt staining the edges

of baseboards and hairballs tumbling
over the hardwoods while Dove and

Swiffer and Mr. Clean isolate in separate
closets. Things do fall apart if we let them.

It doesn't require a pandemic or invasion
or an angry mob unmasked waving

antiquated flags. A president lies
or jokes or conspires; then two brothers

target a store clerk, and soccer moms
drizzle insults upon the teen scooping

their Rocky Road. Someone dropped
a mirror on the floor and hasn't

swept the pieces, yet. A president tells
us it's not his job: it isn't his fault.

I am beginning to believe him.

Half/Full

Half of us are scared of socialists
and who they will make us love.
Half of us are scared of corporations
and what they will make us buy.
Half of us fear the stranger in a hoodie.
Half of us fear our high school friends
and their guns. Half of us are addicted
to porn. Half of us think of cancelling
our internet and closing our minds in a book.
Half of us joke about pussy. Half of us
won't tell our partners what we talk
about on girls' night out. Half of us
study the stock market. Half of us dream
of social security. Half of us giggle
when the grandchildren visit. Half of us
say we don't need nobody. Half of us still
mow our own lawns. Half of us say to hell
with everybody's expectations. Half
of us have quit drinking. Half of us can't
wait till five. Half of us wear a mask
even before we are asked. Half of us
seldom leave a tip. Half of us see red.
Half of us are singing the blues.

Evacuation
after a photograph from Ukraine

The train is leaving the station.
You hear the knocks and clanks

as it jerks into purpose. A boy's
face presses against a window.

Like a rag wiping away a fog,
his hand lifts, forlorn, acquiescent.

You know nothing about him
or his fate, but you want to signal

to him to turn from the blurred
faces of men sending him away,

faces that are already turning back
toward their own desperate duty.

Art
for Bill Jeffers

He told
a story
of carving
a sculpture
from flawless
white stone
long and
sturdy
heavy
like a trunk
of driftwood
a column
maybe
inside
a house
by a window
looking outside
at the sea
it would rise
like a dove
ascending
in a narrow
cage
he chiseled
curls
like cupped
hands
swirls
like O'Keefe's
flowers
whirls
like leaves
in wind
inward twirls

like conch
or ear
the stone
danced
from the floor
levitating
luminescent
poised for
final inspection
then
it tilted
fell
shattered
a hundred
shells
on the carpet
like
remnants
of a wave.

Perusing Hugo

The wonder of it shocks me now.
How is it I'm discovering his poems
in this Virginia library on a rainy
Tuesday morning in the middle of August,
forty years following his death?
I mean, I know. Time and duty. No one
pays us to live our lives in miracles.
Nor can we fish in every stream, wading
into the rush up to our hips, casting
and casting. A damn shame, really.

Ransom
(After Mark: 10:45)

So, here, the fall, again,
my thoughts turn toward God.

If only I remembered
when I uttered that "yes,"

into whatever blank
space the future would be

yawned from. Such casual
tolerance of rebirth's

routine performance. And
so many emeralds

resolved carnelian,
so many bending stem

absolved to brittle stalk.
Into chill autumn wind

voiceless acceptance nods
and bows and looks again

ahead.

Dude for a Day
for my sons

In this photograph, I am standing with my three sons.
You don't know this, but we are in a bowling alley
we rarely visit. You don't know it is my 60th birthday,
but you can see that my long hair, pulled back, is grey.
I am pretending to be Jeff Bridges pretending
to be Jeffrey Lebowsky. It is a silly middle-class thing
to do. You can see I am wearing a black t-shirt

and you can read most of the words asserting
I'm the Dude, Man! and you can see I'm wearing
a gift, a bowling shirt, unbuttoned. Well, you won't
know it is a gift, but it was. Nor will you know,
unless I tell you, but the gifter has had White Russians
stitched across the back of the shirt. Let me tell you
that then and especially today I was and am a little

bothered by the racist implications of that phrase
in America with all the shit that goes down, still. So I am
happy that you can't see that accurate but provocative
movie allusion. Another thing you cannot see
is that everybody has been bowling, drinking Caucasians
by the pitcher-full and eating enchiladas on *watch out,
hot plates!* plates, spicy and sloppy in melting cheese.

My wife, my father-in-law, my niece, family, are all
here, and the best drinking buddies from work, English
professors slumming it in a Cathedral of Pop Culture,
one even wearing aviator glasses like John Goodman's
wounded veteran. It really was a great celebration
of, for me, an important event that captured a small
part of one of my alter-egos, laid-back, care-free,

irresponsible, and careless in the worst of ways.
The next Monday we were all back at work doing
our assigned and, maybe, chosen roles in this big bad
world. Most of this you cannot know if you just
happened to see this photograph. What I hope you
can see is that each son is looking in a different direction,
somewhere ahead. Somewhere in front of them, something,

somebody has their attention as they stand arm-in-arm
with me. This moment will never happen again, exactly
in this way. We will never be the same father and sons.
The things they are looking toward, perhaps not knowing
what they are seeing or thinking they are seeing,
the surprises they cannot imagine, all that lies ahead,
or behind us really, someday, you and me staring into the past.

Epithalamium
for William and Kati

A father stands to read a poem
about love. His first son will be
married today, and all the pleasures
and tests of that vow will open
before him and before the woman
he will devote himself to.

Friends and family, bride and groom
will listen, maybe. But mostly
the deepest, lightest part of themselves
will turn inside and talk to itself,
remembering their moments of greatest joy.
Inside them, between them, around them
twist and tango and jitterbug
the memories and visions of their longing,
and of their longing fulfilled:

Maybe it was a quiet conversation
in a loud and rowdy room
when two hearts wanted nothing more
than to listen to the other's pains and hopes,
or maybe a mountain sunrise hike,
gently holding hands, and astonished
by the silent birth of a new day's beauty,
or maybe it was the first stare
of their fragile naked baby, eyes focused
and, oh, that smile bursting thoughtlessly
at the sight of them. Desire's generous gifts.

So a father stands to read
a poem about love. But it is really
a poem about thanksgiving. Today's

blessing is a tender reawakening
of joy's perennial bounty,
a manifestation of sacred delight.
His son's love, his son's bride's love,
call forth the love that resides in all
of us, sometimes afraid and shy,
but always already present, attentive,
eager to reach out a hand and say yes.

Tourist Trade
Arlington, Virginia

After a long, long day of reminding ourselves
about what being an American is supposed
to mean, you know, the memorials to war dead,

museums with famous painted heads, the chunks of stone
carved with fragments of half-forgotten speeches from time's
retreat, we cross back over the river, Lincoln illuminated,

and turned away, to the rebellious state, tired, cold,
hungry, huddled in our Uberred SUV.
Stop here, my daughter-in-law commands, as we round

a hill, we need snacks. Never surprised at the caprice
of citizens, our driver keeps the car warm
for my wife, shamed by our deplorable appetites,

while the rest of us invade Fort Myer Market,
and fill plastic bags and our underfed
imaginations with cheap California merlot,

Hot Pockets, Cool Ranch Doritos, and Ben and Jerry's
Americone Dream. With a sigh, our driver asks
if we are done, and taking the long way, determines

to drive us past that statue from that old movie,
the one with the people reaching toward the flag,
and back to our suites purchased on credit and points.

What He Knows of Sunlight

His wife berates him
for "posturing" naked
before the uncurtained

windows while he dresses
for his professional day.
What if the neighbors

were stealing glimpses
of his manhood hidden
in layers of belly fat?

Impossible, he says.
Has he ever enjoyed
the vision of the nude

crone next door emerging
from her morning shower,
toweling writhing hair,

glistening in unreflected
sunlight falling upon
the bend of her wrinkled neck?

Sacrificial
three images from "Araby"

His innocent eyes widened
into confusion as she twirled
the silver bracelet around
her narrow wrists. Round
and round slowly, thoughtlessly,
temptingly, her thin fingers
rubbing a dull stain on to her skin.

He ached to reach out to stop
the spinning. Oh, what would he
have paid? The coins from Sunday's
salver clinked in his imagination.
The street lights hummed in violet
dusk, and he wondered why
adults haven't called him in yet.

Holding On
from a scene in the novel *A Place on Earth*

I have been reading about a flood,
not the kind that rises slowly
as if the backyard were a clogged

shower gradually filling, but the sudden,
shocking howling rush of an avalanche,
like God's firehose abruptly unwrenched.

And I have been thinking about
my garden, so dry this summer, cracked
soil and droopy leaves, small bitter fruit.

I could have seen it coming and placed
the soakers in right places at right times
and let water flow. But I kept hoping

for rain. Now I want to drive somewhere,
far away, and be shocked by things
I have never seen, never even heard of.

Cloudy Day

It should have been easier
to lift from the chair and walk
the neighborhood today. Stillness
insisted that lives be at ease,
and almost I did not listen.
But once in the street, descending

from the house toward the park,
I felt the flannelled air of gray
sky hug me, enwrap and enrapt
me, steadying something very
wobbly inside. What if I had not
seen my gardening friend Cathy

kneeled in her front lawn kindly
planting bulbs for the coming year,
had not heard the voices of young men
playing basketball rise to enchant
me in their sweetly masculine
exuberance, or couples laughing

on a porch, drinking wine, playing
an old folk tune on their guitars,
the rising minor key chiming
the falling leaves, carnelian,
gamboge, and maroon? How emptied
would I have remained, bereft

of pots of xanthic mums alighting
front steps, or jagged-toothed pumpkins
smiling as I sauntered by, giant
sycamore leaves crusting and crackling

under my feet? Turning the final
corner near home, the neighbor's

wild ageratum misted her lawn
in wistful mauve starbursts. And this
was fifteen minutes I could have
lost, negligent, when tender
majesty was so close, and
beauty's comfort offered so near.

Toward Atonement
three images from the novel *Jack*

A good first step is to purchase a houseplant,
say, a geranium, and place it on the dusted desk

by the window of your shabby room. Ah,
that afternoon light flat upon the open palm

of its leaves! Tend to it, like a child, lean
close and smell the citrus of its happy innocence.

Next, once you know you will not kill
the bloom, find the tiny book your father gifted

you before you fled, so many pages with folded
corners and question marks. Feel once again

the press of his hand on your knee, the sounding
of his fear for you, sinking, sinking, in his always

forgiving watery eyes. Retrieve that favored
passage and ask those perfect words to haunt you

again, and again. It is you, not he, who dreads
the returning. The shutter, the quaking in your chest,

are aftershocks of a greater distant slippage.
Finally, pick up from the floor the letter, soiled

and stained by its long journey to you. Yes, now.
Now you commit, before the tear and the unfolding.

Acknowledgements

I am grateful to the editors and publishers of the journals and anthologies where the following poems were previously published.

"The Dying Leaves," in *Maufris*
"Love Song from Country of Memory," in *Through the Fire*
"Cancer," in *Icarus*
"Grieving for My Parents," in *Through the Fire*
"The Drawing," in *Sulphur River Literary Review*
"The Garden," in *Enkidu*
"The Light through the Peaks," in MAN! and *Through the Fire*
"The Open Hand," in MAN!
"Found Things," in *Is This Forever, or What?: Poems and Paintings from Texas,* and *Purpose, Pattern, and Process*
"Endings," in *Enkidu*
"Searching the Parking Lot for a Poem," in *Sulphur River Literary Review* and in *Best Texas Writing I*
"The Rose's Thorns," in *Concho River Review*
"290 West," in The *Beatest State in the Union: An Anthology of Beat Texas Writing*
"Absolution," in *Di-Verse City 2005*
"Hamlet," in *Cider Press Review*
"Black Bowl with Apples on Old Table Cloth," in *Di-Verse City Too*
"If You Should Ever Return," in *Di-Verse City 2006*
"The Way Things Go," in *Concho River Review*
"Soul Mates," in *Di-Verse City 2004*
"These are things I've been wanting to tell you," in *Di-Verse City* and in *The Great American Wise Ass Anthology*
"An Animal Speaks of Speaking on Christmas Day," in *Windhover*
"Late Night," in *Feeding the Crow*
"The Angel of Santa Maria," in *At the River's Side* and in *Feeding the Crow*
"Setting Them Down," in *Feeding the Crow*

"A Dream of Grace," in *Feeding the Crow*
"More Metaphors," in *Feeding the Crow*
"The Laying on of Hands," in *Feeding the Crow*
"Dark Night on Deck Upstairs," in *Rose and Thorn*
"The Other Writers Block," in *Teaching English in the Two-Year College* and in *The Great American Wise Ass Anthology*
"Midlife Christmas," in *Angel Face*
"Six Motets," in *The Texas Observer*
"Product Reliability," in *Houston Poetry Festival* and in *Blue Hole*
"Listening and Knowing Where to Look," in *Timber Creek Review*
"After Hades, Always Persephone," in *Sulphur River Literary Review*
"Weekend Forecast," in *Texas Poetry Calendar*, and in *Big Land, Big Sky, Big Hair: The Best of the Texas Poetry Calendar*
"Dawning," in *Compton Review*
"Ice Storm," in *Compton Review*
"Burn Ban," in *RE: Arts and Letters*
"The Upper Room," in *Windhover*
"This Easter," in *Di-Verse City 2009*
"It is not that I," in *Windhover*
"Sometimes I cannot, "in *Windhover* and in *New Poetry Appreciation*
"Speed Limit," in *Concho River Review*
"Pedestal," in *Ropes Literary Journal*
"The Lure," in *descant*
"Scene from the Movie Diva," in *Writing Texas*
"Summer Returns to Texas," in *Concho River Review* and in *The Great American Wise Ass Anthology*
"The Tab," in *Agave: A Celebration of Tequila in Story, Song, Poetry, Essay, and Graphic Art*
"Three Teslas," in *Five Friends, Sunday Afternoons* and in *Endlessly Rocking: Poems in Honor of Walt Whitman's 200th Birthday*

"Mayberry Sequence," in *Writing Texas*
"The High Shelf," in *Voices de la Luna*, and in *Five Friends, Sunday Afternoons*
"Old Men on Tuesday Mornings," *Red River Review*
"Arroyo Sunset," in *Texas Poetry Calendar*
"Deep End," in *In Between Hangovers*
"From What Planet," in *Raw Paw*
"Ghost Story," in *Texas Poetry Calendar* and in *Best of the Texas Poetry Calendar*
"Tourist Trade," in *Written in Arlington*
"SOS," in *Tejas Covidos*
"Epithalamium," as "Always Already" in *Five Friends, Sunday Afternoons*
"Cloudy Day," in *Equinox* and in *Poetry Society of Virginia Centennial Anthology*
"Toward Atonement," in *Poetry Society of Virginia Centennial Anthology*

About the Author

Lyman Grant lives in the Shenandoah Valley. For four and a half decades, he taught at Austin Community College and served in various administrative roles including Dean of Arts and Humanities. He is the editor of *New Growth: Contemporary Short Fiction from Texas*, *Short Fiction: Classic and Contemporary*, and *The Letters of Roy Bedichek*. He served as book review editor of *The Texas Humanist* and fiction editor for *Brazos River Review* and published essays and reviews in *Texas Observer*, *Texas Books in Review*, *The Langdon Review*, *Creative Pulse*, and *Dallas Morning News*. With John Lee and Sharon Adams, he founded and edited MAN!, a quarterly magazine devoted to men's issues. His poems have appeared in numerous journals and anthologies and in several volumes of poetry, including *The Road Home, As Long as We Need, Old Men on Tuesday Mornings*, and *2018: Found Poems and Weather Reports*. He is married and the father of three sons.